I Have a Voice

DOLORES ROSE

ISBN: 1496012208
ISBN 13: 9781496012203
Library of Congress Control Number: 2014903487
CreateSpace Independent Publishing Platform
North Charleston, South Carolina

I dedicate this memoir to those individuals who still carry the burden of their secrets and who desperately want to relieve their souls. In sharing my secrets with you, I desire to offer hope.

I am revealing my secrets to you on a brutally honest level. I found out I am not alone.

Part Two of my memoir is my spiritual fantasy. This is not a fantasy to me. It is what I feel and believe. I present it in this manner because of what exists.

There is the rage.

There is the anger.

There is the hurt.

There is the other side of the story.

There is compassion.

There is forgiveness.

There is gratitude.

There is healing.

There is transformation.

There is freedom.

"Self-conquest is the greatest of all victories."
—Plato

ACKNOWLEDGMENTS

I WANT TO thank my grandmother, whose unconditional love for me gave me the strength to become the person I am today.

I would like to thank my middle uncle and his wife, who extended their hands to me and brought me out of the darkness into the light.

I want to thank all the actors in my play of life. Your roles were exquisitely performed. I give you a standing ovation.

My most supreme gratitude goes to those who gave me the most suffering and pain.

Yes, you brought me to suffering, but doing that led me to another S word: spirituality.

I want to thank my addictions—alcohol, drugs, and food. You helped me survive the most horrible times of my life.

You, my weaknesses, brought me through recovery and to my highest blessings and strengths.

I wish to thank the defense mechanisms that I developed to help me survive.

I wish to thank my family who believe in me and my friends who are always there for me. I especially thank Judy Ouellette, who says, "We are sisters from another mother."

Also, I thank the songwriters and musicians whose songs comforted me through difficult times. Your words offered hope and motivation to me—and still do.

Where would I be without my Monday afternoon twelve-step group, who has loved me and continues to love me back to health?

The support and encouragement helped me see the greater picture and stay focused on my writing.

The best is for last: I wish to thank my beloved husband, Jim. His love for me enabled me to find trust, loyalty, and support in the arms of a man. You were my cool drink in my parched desert of loneliness. My delicious intermezzo, with just one look your love was revealed. I miss the goodness of your heart.

I am truly grateful that I was blessed with your love.

CONTENTS

FOREWORD

DOLORES ROSE IS an example of a person whose innocence was taken away in childhood by an adult who took advantage of her. She worked hard to develop the self-esteem of which she had been robbed. She worked hard to develop a voice of her own. She worked hard to learn to assert herself so that she would no longer be another person's prey. In *I Have a Voice*, she describes how she went from being easy prey as a child to the confident woman who has chosen to write this book to help others in similar circumstances. I applaud her courage, her resilience, and her work toward healing herself and, ultimately, the world.

—Dr. Steven Diamond, psychiatrist

PART ONE: THE PERPETRATORS ARE BROUGHT TO AN AWARENESS OF THEIR DEEDS

DOLORES: HER INNER child is referred to as the Innocent Lamb. The image of Christ holding the baby lamb invokes tender emotion in me. It reminds me that all children are born innocent. The inner child is innocent.

Dolores: The Adult Wizard is not dressed in a special costume, wearing a tall multicolored hat or holding a magic wand. I use the term *Wizard* to describe the adult Dolores. The Wizard has the magic of knowing the inner child, the little girl, Dolores. The Wizard knows her hurts, her disappointments, the abandonment, the incest, and the addictions. The Wizard will speak for the Innocent Lamb, confronting all those people who have damaged her. She will speak the emotions of the innocent inner child, who had no voice to confront the perpetrators.

The Perpetrators:

1. Mother
2. Beast (Molester)
3. Aunt
4. Father Uncle
5. Father

PART TWO: MY SPIRITUAL FANTASY

The Chamber
The Hall of Recollection
The House of Mirrors
The Mansion of Truth and Jubilation
The Tower of the Sacred and Divine

THE CHAMBER

ALL PERPETRATORS WERE summoned and escorted to the Chamber.

The Chamber was a circular room joined to the Hall of Recollection. The perpetrators arrived. They sat on the beautiful couches that were built into the wall. The guide who welcomed them was bombarded by many questions. They wondered why they were summoned; was this a trial with a judge and jury? The guide laughed and said, "This is not a trial. It is simply a recollection of the past."

After hearing this, many became very anxious and sweaty. The guide encouraged them to partake of the sandwiches, sweets, and drinks provided. The woman who happened to be a nun and the man who happened to be a priest sat together—the nun saying her rosary, the priest reading a spiritual book.

Mother, Aunt, Father, and Father Uncle were together waiting and wondering. The Beast and the Vulture conversed and laughed. The Last Secret was very pale and sat alone.

Finally, it was time to proceed to the Hall of Recollection. Mother was summoned first.

The Hall of Recollection

The Hall of Recollection was a room with a high ceiling. The cherry-wood floor was so polished that neither a speck of dust nor a scuff mark was visible. The front of the room was crowded with various scrolls and tapestries. There was a feeling that a higher authority was in the room but was not visible. A raised platform adorned the middle of the room. The platform held a straight-backed chair that was not comfortable. It was not meant to be. A small television screen was attached to the arm of the chair. On the other side stood a beautiful antique desk with legs of cut wood. A crystal water pitcher with matching glasses was arranged on the desk. There was a box of very soft tissues; smelling salts; and, toward the end of the desk, beautifully arranged pink roses. They brought softness to the room. The pink rose denoted love.

In the back of the room stood a similar desk. The Innocent Lamb and the Wizard were seated there. The Innocent Lamb wore her Holy Communion dress. The Wizard was dressed in a beautifully tailored gray suit. She wore a bold red V-neck sweater with cap sleeves. Her jewelry was circular gold earrings, a gold watch, and a sapphire stone ring. For comfort, she wore black patent leather shoes with a low heel.

All was ready to begin. The Wizard requested the perpetrators to listen only.

MOTHER

I CALL YOU first, but I write about you last.

I called you first because you hurt me the most.

I was named after my grandmother. Her Italian name was Adolorato. The closest name in English was Dolores. Was it a coincidence that my birth happened on the feast day of Our Lady of Sorrows? Artists depicted the Blessed Virgin in paintings with seven swords piercing her heart.

My name, Dolores, means sorrow. I grew to hate that name. *Hate* is a strong word, a word I have erased from my present-day vocabulary.

It was a Thursday afternoon at 4:02 p.m., September 15, 1949. The doctor announced the baby was coming out breach (feet first). Prepare for a C-section! I turned at the last moment to spare you the C-section surgery.

We never bonded. From my birth to your death, we never bonded. I came from you, but I never felt I was part of you. I was told I cried and cried. You took me to Grandma's house, around the corner from your apartment, and there, I stopped crying. At first, you brought me to Grandma's in the morning. Within a short time, you left me with Grandma. She took over your responsibility as a mother. Grandma raised me and gave me unconditional love (my saving grace).

You, Mother, didn't want me. It was as simple as that. I had feelings of abandonment. At that young age, I did not know the word to describe those feelings. You worked in a shoe factory. You brought me Mary Jane shoes—that is the only good thing I remember about you from early childhood.

What mother tells her little girl with pretty ribbons and banana curls that she was found in a garbage can with coffee grinds? The stork story would have been kinder.

From that moment on, I felt like an alien. Where did I belong?

Because of that tale, I started to become a people pleaser. I felt I had to act a certain way—a way that was expected for me to be loved—for me to feel safe in this family.

After a while, interpreting other people's body language became easy. I did whatever was expected of me. An uneasy feeling separated me. I was different, but I was desperate to be a part of things. I was the frightened child (the Innocent Lamb) who wanted her mother to want and love her.

I am asking you, Mother:

> How could a mother hear a heartbeat,
> Feel a kick,
> And then discard this precious gift from God
> Like a nothing,
> Like she didn't exist?

Your harsh tongue hurt me on so many instances.

One morning, I ran upstairs to watch you put on your makeup. You took hours getting ready for work. Still, you were always late. I sat on the toilet seat watching you. You put a beauty mark on your right cheek with a brown pencil.

I said, "When I grow up, I will not use all that makeup."

You turned to me and said, "Go downstairs, you brat."

With tears in my eyes, I ran to Grandma.

At the age of eight, I slipped on the cement basement floor. I fell on my right arm. It really hurt, so I ran to you. Grandma was not home. You were cleaning the beautiful kitchen floor. It matched the kitchen table, with white tile carefully cut out in certain places with golden leaves. There was a pink refrigerator and pink stove. All were purchased on special order from California. The stove had a grill in the middle where one could easily cook pancakes and eggs. There was one problem. These were for show, not for use.

So, there I was, crying, asking for your help. Your response was to tap me on the head with the mop stick. I stepped on the wet floor. Then you said, "Go wait for your grandmother to come home." That was the last time I came to you for anything.

At this point, Mother sobbed uncontrollably. Reaching for the tissues, she saw her child, Dolores, through the TV screen on the arm of the chair. There she was, the little girl at her bedside, leaning with her right arm on top of the bed. Her head was hung low. Her waist-length braid hung loosely down her back. Mother kept crying.

There would be no break in the recollection. Had the little girl experienced a break from her suffering?

Yes, Mother, your rejection of me was a sword that pierced my heart.

When Grandma came home, she immediately looked at my arm. She made a paste with whipped eggs. She placed it firmly on my arm. It was held with a facecloth. This was an old-time remedy. She berated you in Italian. It was too fast for me to understand. I knew she was yelling at you for not taking care of me.

We went to the doctor. He said I had a broken elbow cap. If it wasn't fixed, the arm would never grow. When I heard that I had to go to the hospital, I screamed for Grandma to come and stay with me. To quiet me, you promised you would get me a dog when I got out of the hospital. I believed you. What dog? It was a stuffed poodle that could be pulled along the ground. So much for your promise. Another disappointment.

My sister was born when I was twelve years old. You said to me, "This one is mine." I guess that left me out.

Your words were arrows to my heart.

When I was fifteen, I was "taken" by the Beast. Father's stepsister insisted the way the Beast looked at me was not right. You looked quite concerned when you asked me, "Did he do anything to you? I'll kill him!"

But how could I trust you? You were never there for me. Grandma passed before my fourteenth birthday. Ever since her passing, I felt completely on my own.

Your attitude was depressing for all. You wanted more and more. Gratitude was not part of your mind-set.

We shared a weight problem. You took me with you to my first experience at the diet doctor. He gave me shots and pills to lose weight. We went every week. I loved the feeling those pills gave me—a feeling that I desired on a daily basis. This craving was my introduction to my addiction to speed.

Admit it, Mother—you didn't love me. To love is a verb—a verb denotes action. Therefore, by your actions and by your words—and lack of words—you did not love me.

Did you know I searched for a mother's love throughout my life?

Things I saw on TV would move me to tears. I watched the Dove soap commercial with three generations of women—the grandmother, mother, and daughter—and I longed for that belonging.

The one that got to me the most was the lioness and her cubs. The lioness left her two cubs in a safe place so she could hunt for food. One cub strayed to the water hole. She did not sense the danger of the crocodile. She was too young. Amazingly, she crossed to the small mound of dirt. The lioness heard her cry for help. Immediately, the lioness rushed to the aid of her cub.

The lioness paced back and forth. The camera lens captured the anxiety in the lines of her body and the more-than-concerned look on her face. Wanting to follow the adrenaline shooting through her, the lioness let her wisdom tell her to wait for the right timing. She dashed across the watering hole with no thought of her own life. She grabbed her cub in her mouth and raced to the safe side. She licked her cub.

Mother, I was never your cub.

The worst was when Father died. You cried for him and felt guilty for his death. You would stay up all night eating and sleep late the next day. You took Valium after Valium. There was a good reason to be afraid. The house was about to go into foreclosure.

You prayed and prayed to St. Anthony for help. But, Mother, you took no action.

And yet your prayers were answered. Someone bought the house, and we finally had some money to pay the bills.

But my sister was going to get married. There was not enough money to pay for everything. You didn't listen to me when I told you we must pay the taxes. It was more important for my sister to have a car and a wedding.

After the wedding, the newlyweds moved out of the country.

You and I were left to discard all the furniture and do a clean sweep of the house. In November, we moved into your sister's basement—a basement I dreaded. The walls knew the story that others could not or would not see. The Beast had started molesting me here. I never wanted to see that couch again.

As you slept alongside me in our separate twin beds, all I heard was your snoring. It wasn't snoring. Your chest was filling with fluid. You took your medicine when you wanted to—when everything turned critical.

This time was different. You were so overweight that your feet were swollen. You wore open-toed slippers—even in winter. You took the dogs out and froze with your housedress and sweater. That winter would be your last.

You told me you would be dying soon. But why tell me? Call your daughter. See if she will come running home.

When your daughter came home for Christmas 1980, you looked so happy. Why didn't you go home with her? I can hear your voice protesting, "What, and leave you?" You were never with me. I was always alone.

You had a new term to define me. It was, "Poor Dolores, poor Dolores. She has no one."

Just before you passed, you went to the Times Square Store because your daughter had to get her supplies to take back with her. You walked outside in those slippers with the dog and your sister by your side. I never saw you leave because I was sleeping downstairs. I never went to breakfast.

Then the Beast summoned me. He said, "Your mother is dead." Just like that—with no emotion in his voice. You passed in the car, the dog by your side, while your daughter and sister were inside the store. They came out and saw policemen by the car. They knew something was wrong, but what?

The dog was still there and knew the whole story. You were already dead as an ambulance carried you away.

So many emotions were swirling around in me—pity, anger, guilt for the relief. Your death felt so freeing. I didn't have to hear you praising your daughter while I was so near. It was all so very sad. You were dressed in the gown that you bought for your daughter's wedding. You looked peaceful, and, yes, I was glad you were dead. Feeling this emotion would tear me apart because I knew I should not be glad. You were my mother.

After the funeral everyone went back to their lives. I went back to the basement, the walls, the couch, the Beast, the Last Secret, and all—back to the basement to settle your affairs, to keep peace with the others. While everyone went on with their lives, I was stuck in the basement with the "stuff" that wasn't mine.

The Beast complained about Sister's car. I had to sell it because—could you believe it?—parking it there could crack the cement. So sell it and get it out of here, the faster the better.

I sold the car, but that wasn't enough. Now Sister's boxes under the pool table, which they said she could leave, just became too much stuff. "Get rid of that stuff. Don't you know that brings bugs?"

Please, God, help me get out of here!

Just one more thing, Mother.

Many years later, after going to therapy, I was sitting opposite my girlfriend. She told me about her weekend and how she went to a psychic fair with a friend of hers. I started to feel very uncomfortable. There was that hole in my gut. I started wondering why I hadn't been invited. She knew I loved to go to things like that. While my friend was talking to me, I was having an internal conversation. My friend could do whatever and go with whomever she wanted. Why was I feeling left out? Oh, that was what it was: my deep core issue of abandonment. This was not happening to me now. This was part of my past. The abandonment of my mother. I could let it go.

From years of therapy, I am grateful to be able to sit with the feeling and follow it through. This, Mother, was your legacy to me: abandonment!

Mommy, why didn't you want me?

BEAST (MOLESTER)

FRIDAY MORNING, FEBRUARY 19, 2009, 3:00 a.m.

I've been writing most of the day. I can't stop. I put down my pen around 11:00 p.m. and took a wonderful bath, trying to relax, but I can't get to sleep.

The molester keeps appearing in my head. So I get up and put on my robe, go downstairs to my writing area, and prepare to face the devil. The images running across my mind's eye are too vivid. God, please, I don't want to go back there. Not this way. I don't want to look at every detail, every detail of the loss of my virginity. You keep telling me I must go back to be healed. Did I say I wanted to be healed? Of course I want to be healed, but I don't want to go back.

But wait. Yes, there I am. It's a motel. It looks like a corner I am being rushed in. Oh, because I am a minor, I walk down the back steps. No, God, I don't want to see this; it's too much.

There I am.
I'm naked on the bed.
He is over me.
He is trying to put that penis between my
legs but not to go all the way,
Just to rub.
There he has it.
As he comes closer to me,
I turn my face.
I can't look.

This isn't love.
I feel shame.
Oh, leave me alone.
Grandma, Grandma, save me,
Save me from this Beast.
It's going in.
It hurts.
He says, "I went too far."
That's my virginity you're taking.
That's for me to give,
Not to be taken by you.
You beast!
You bastard!
Why can't you just leave me alone?

I want my grandma. How could you leave me, Grandma? There's no one I can turn to, no one to listen, no one to believe, no one to trust. What will it become—a secret? A dirty, dark secret! God, are you there? How could you bring me back to that day? What do I hear? *My child—yes, you were a child—it wasn't your fault; you did nothing wrong. You did nothing wrong. You did nothing wrong. You did nothing wrong. You are not to blame. Stop blaming yourself.*

But, Jesus, he took my self-worth. How will another man love me? I am damaged, damaged by the Beast—a dirty rag.

No, my child, you are not damaged. You are a child of God. You are my child, and you are saved by me.

I never felt saved by God till many, many years later.

From the time I was ten, I was tainted. We were at a wedding, a cousin's wedding on my father's side. The Molester, who was drinking, pulled me onto his lap. His right hand slipped under my dress and up between my legs. It happened in a flash; it happened so fast I didn't know it was happening. I pulled myself off his lap, but it was too late. Already my body felt different, especially down there.

He touched my vessel, and my light went out.

Oh, make it not have happened! He touched, yes, he did touch me, and now I am not the same.

Should I tell Grandma?

No, I'll keep it to myself.

What would I tell her?

I knew nothing—even when I got my period. I was twelve years old. It was a Sunday, the day before my sister was born, my only sister. I was in the bathroom. I went to wipe myself, and there it was…blood. I screamed, "I'm bleeding!"

Grandma, Mother, and Aunt ran in from the backyard. They told me, "This is your period." My aunt said I was a woman now. "Stay away from boys," she warned me, though why, I never knew.

"Stay away from boys," I thought resentfully. "Keep your husband away from me."

They gave me a belt and a Kotex pad, and that was that. That was my story about the birds and the bees.

I do not have a time line for the sexual incidents that occurred between us. I will relate what I do remember.

After that first touch when I was ten, nothing happened for a while. You became my friend—telling me about the importance of a college education. No one else cared whether I went to college or not. You were my confidant, and I trusted you.

But then it started up, this time with a single touch. When you touched my breasts, my body responded. It betrayed me. Why was I getting wet between my legs? You went no further. There was the day you came in from the pool with only a towel wrapped around your waist. As you entered the room, I saw something sticking straight out underneath the towel. The telephone rang. You turned away to answer it, and I jumped from the couch and ran outside. Whatever that was, it frightened me.

When I was twelve years old and attending a birthday party, one of the games we played was spin the bottle. A boy that I liked kissed me for the first time. You showed me a different type of kiss. What did you call it? A French kiss. You darted your tongue into my mouth and even sucked my tongue. And I just allowed it to happen.

For many years, I held myself responsible. I blamed myself—it was all my fault. Why didn't I push you away? Why didn't I tell the truth about you when I was questioned?

You took advantage of my circumstances. My grandmother died; she was my only protector. I was so sad and lonely. You took advantage of me, you beast. You said you loved me, but you treated me like garbage. You told me I had a gold mine between my legs.

For a time, I actually fell in love with you. I looked at you as if you were my boyfriend. I even wanted to be married to you. How could I have such feelings?

The guilt—the shame I bore—I bore most of my life.

I've had endless dreams of me scrubbing sheets in the shower in the basement. I sit with the water running over me, washing the sheets. They are always white sheets, and I am always scrubbing them. Do you know how many times I've had this nightmare of a dream? Forget about the dream—a dream is something you can wake up from. How could I wake up to my life? What life? The life of being a victim. The life of being used time and time and time again. You even approached my mother with that dick of yours.

One afternoon, my mother told me you approached her with your "tool" ready to hammer away. She refused your advances. She couldn't believe it. Three months later, she was dead. I was still trapped in that basement.

You were creative with the names you made up for me. The Cuckoo Bird, because I started going to therapy. The Dust Collector. And the funniest of all (to you and the Last Secret), Mattress on Back. I took it all: the sex, the names. What were those phrases you told me all the time? "I want to pleasure you" and "the quickie."

I was smoking three packs of cigarettes a day. I was a full-blown alcohol and speed addict. I decided I wanted to give up cigarettes. I thought if I could give up cigarettes, I could give up drinking. I sat across from you at the kitchen table and said, "This is my last cigarette."

You smiled and said, "Oh, you can't stop smoking."

After fifteen minutes went by, you took your cigarette and put it to my lips. "Here, take mine. You can't stop."

Want to see me stop? Well, I did stop—cold turkey. But you, you smoked until you died. Even when you had cancer, you kept puffing away.

It was only after I moved out of your reach that the molesting stopped. I was thirty-one, going to therapy, when I began to understand what happened to me. I was molested. I really didn't know. I looked that word up in the dictionary:

- To annoy, interfere with, or meddle with so as to trouble or harm.
- To make improper advances to, esp. of a sexual nature.

That definition is too tame to me. A bee buzzing around is annoying. A molester is a killer—a killer of spirit and potential.

I got sober in 1983 at the age of thirty-three. Five years later, I was engaged to a wonderful man. I stayed overnight and slept in Aunt's bedroom with her. You slept in the other room—you and your cancer. Aunt left for the beauty parlor. After so many years, I never thought you would come near me again. I was wrong. You never got help or even acknowledged your sins.

I was in bed. I turned, and there you were. Your robe opened in the front, that stiff prick was ready for action. You came near me and whispered, "You always did it for me." This time I pushed you away. I told you that what happened between us was wrong. I told you, "Don't you ever come near me again."

Did you apologize? You said nothing. You walked out. I spoke with the voice of the Innocent Lamb. I kept my anger at bay. I was pathetically polite when I confronted you.

When I first found out that I had been molested, I wanted to kill you. I wanted to go upstairs, put my two thumbs under your throat, and strangle you. Watch as every breath left your lungs and your body hung limp. With the rage I had inside, I had no doubt that I could have killed you. Strangling is a crime of passion. What did I do instead? I went out and destroyed myself with alcohol, sex, and drugs.

Do I care about your background and the things that happened to you that made you the Beast? No, I do not. You had a choice: the light or the darkness. You chose the darkness and brought that darkness upon everyone who came in contact with you.

I was a child.
I was not to blame.
I was innocent.
You were the adult.

It was 9/11. The word *violation* stuck in my throat. I was violated, violated, violated. America was violated. The innocence of my country was taken like a virgin in her bed. She bleeds!

As for me, I go back to therapy, needing antidepressants and anti-anxiety medication.

Then, there was the movie. It was after my husband died. Sitting alone, I watched as a close-up of the leading actor's face caught me by surprise. It was his nose. It was the Beast's nose. I was no longer watching the movie; I was watching the movie in my head. The Beast was on top of me. I saw his face, and there was that nose. I ran from the theater with tears in my eyes, wondering if I would ever be rid of the haunting of the Beast.

His body language revealed his thoughts. He had just about enough of this "recollection." Innocent, with a body like hers. That little bitch—she asked for it, and he gave it to her. Why was she making such a big production about it now? He wrestled in his chair. It was not his conscience. He needed a cigarette.

I am not through with you yet.

My subconscious summoned you to my dream state.

This time you come into my bedroom dressed in dark clothing; you look very old and sad. You lie on my husband's side of the bed. You lie above the covers. I lie under the covers, and I am naked, white sheets covering me. I tell you to go. *Now—I do not want to do anything with you.* I say that Mother and Aunt will be back soon to clean the house. I do not want you here to start trouble. You get up, put on a loose beige raincoat. You leave, but you leave three muddy footprints on my rug as you exit the room. The pillow has a stain from the back of your head. I feel the stain is the mark you have left on me—a mark that this writing will wash away for good.

Go; I give you no power, no power over me.

My Vision for You in Hell

You are in a puppy mill crate,
Bars surround the crate.
You can see all around you.
You are naked,
On all fours with the foul smell of your feces and urine.
The size of the crate will not allow you to stand.
Outside the crate,
The most beautiful females
Parade their wares with their
"Gold mine between their legs."
Fortunately for them,
The only thing
You can put
Your dick in
Is your hand.

AUNT

My earliest memories of you are ones of affection and caring. You were a couple of years younger than my real mother. In my mind, you took her place.

I remember the Italian songs you sang and your beautiful voice. You loved to wear wide-brimmed hats. I thought you were so beautiful. I wanted to be just like you. You were both my aunt and godmother. I gaze at the picture of you and Father Uncle at my baptism; both of you were smiling. You looked happy to be my godparents.

We shared the same bedroom. Before you went to work, you would make me a bottle. Sometimes it tasted so good that I would ask you to make me another. You always did—even though you might be late for work.

You loved to dance, and you took me to Star Time Studio. I loved it. I remember the tap dancing, tumbling (which I didn't like), and ballet (which I loved). I remember at the end of each class we would form a line and, like a train, dance out of the class. Once the door opened, there you were waiting for me like a proud parent. You smiled and took my hand, and off we went to the toy store. I could always choose what I wanted. There was no question of cost—whatever I wanted, I got.

I remember the paper doll cutouts. I loved to play with them, but I asked you to cut them out for me. I could never stay within the lines. At night, we would say a prayer to our guardian angel. "Angel of God, my guardian dear…" After that we did our leg exercises. I can remember our bedroom very well.

How can I ever forget about my banana curls? You would set my hair in pin curls, two bobby pins held each curl in place. Grandma had a parakeet named Perry. She taught him to drink from a glass. Perry loved to sit on my head, removing each bobby pin and throwing them on the floor. You would tell me to sit still as your performed your magic on my hair. Oh, the things I remember.

When I made my First Holy Communion, you and Middle Uncle stood in for my real mother and father, who never showed up.

You had a good job, and your boss promoted you. It was here that you met the man you married (the Beast). I remember the night you left to get married. Grandma did not want you to marry him. Regardless, you walked out with him and traveled upstate to get married by a justice of the peace.

I cried and cried when you left. You meant so much to me. I loved you very much. You sent me two postcards from Florida while you were on your honeymoon.

Soon afterward, Grandma received a phone call from you stating the Beast was treating you badly. You were pregnant with your first child. Your brothers were ready to come over and teach the Beast a lesson. Grandma advised them not to interfere. Later, when I was older, you told me about this incident yourself. You shared so much of your life story with me. You were the middle child and rebellious. So many ordinary childhood activities were forbidden. You took your chances, defying the rules, like the time you went roller skating. But there was always the consequence of a beating. Grandma hit you with the shaving strap. I saw the strap. Grandpa used it to shave. I found it difficult to believe that Grandma hit you because Grandma was so good to me.

A talent scout went to your school. You were chosen because of your talent in dancing and singing. Your dream was smashed because Grandma forbade it.

The saddest story you ever told me was about Johnny. Johnny, so gentle, was your first love. You and Johnny were engaged to be married. You had your engagement party. Johnny got sick with an ear infection that ultimately caused his death. I don't think you ever healed from his loss. Johnny gave me a five-dollar gold piece, which I still cherish to this day. You told me he used to tickle my feet.

Sometimes when you reminisced, you would take out a maroon wooden box containing his love letters. He called you "kitten." You were his kitten, and he loved your "cat" eyes. You wore his diamond on your hand.

We shared the same taste in clothing and shoes. Everyone thought that you were my mother. We looked so much alike.

After the birth of your first child, things started changing between us. I was the same, but you started changing. The secrets were starting. When you bought me something, you would follow it by saying, "Don't tell my daughter I got you this." I wondered why not.

Then the hatbox incident happened. For my birthday, you gave me a plaid hatbox with my initials on it. When you were visiting Grandma, you borrowed the hatbox to bring clothes back home. I loaned it to you thinking I would get it back. You kept it.

When your second child was born, you told me stories about going upstate with your two children and the Beast. You said the Beast would go out drinking and having fun while you stayed back with the kids, listening to the sounds of the crickets. Your heart beat faster from the darkness outside and your fear of bugs.

Later, you told me you had to get tough to handle the Beast. You had to find your voice. Yes, you did get tough. To me, that toughness was not you, the person I knew and loved.

That time when you questioned me, the Beast was one step ahead of you (being the expert beast that he was). He told me, "If she asks you anything about us, just deny, deny, deny." He didn't want trouble with you. This was my introduction into lying and denying.

Why did I go along with it? The tone of your voice and the way you looked at me told me I would be blamed. So I lied to you. When you asked, "Are you doing anything with my husband?" I said, "No, how can you ever think that of me?" I wanted to tell you the truth, but, Aunt, what would you have done with the truth? When you know the truth, action is required. Would you have thrown out the Beast? Would the Beast have told the truth? Wasn't he so charming when he needed to be? How could I say this to you? Thus, my body and mind became soaked in guilt and shame.

When I said I was going to the library, the Beast picked me up and brought me to a motel. It was there that he took my virginity. I will spare you the earlier molestations that led up to the big bang. Now what are you going to do about it? Nothing.

I knew I made the right decision. During my first year in college, I received a letter from you. You said, "I knew you had a crush on the Beast and would grow out of it." Oh, I see—it was a teenage crush that started at the age of ten. Well, Aunt, if that gives you peace of mind, so be it. Perhaps I should have sent you the Beast's letters with the lovely four-letter words he used to describe my body. I have a better one.

I went back to college after one of the breaks. My period was late. I told the Beast. He sent me a white square box with black round pills. I was to take these pills to bring on my period. It worked! It was frightening to think that I could have his child. Again, I would have to lie. But for what?

I guess you didn't know that a molester is a sick person. It could be the result of childhood trauma. Maybe he was molested as well.

I always thought I was the only one the Beast molested. But there could have been others. I didn't know what happened to me. I only learned the word *molestation* after a few sessions of therapy at the age of thirty-one! That was the first time I let this secret out. It was inside of me, destroying my life.

Do you have any idea of the damage the Beast did to me both sexually and emotionally? I had no self-worth. All my dreams—all my dreams of getting a good education, being a doctor, and supporting myself—were torn from me. What was left? Loneliness and suffering. How you stayed with that beast your whole life is beyond me.

I felt you took your misplaced anger out on me. Deep down inside, you knew the truth. It was all so confusing to me. At your house, you would prepare feasts of food. You placated everyone's tastes, and your table was always set so eloquently. At Thanksgiving, small wrapped boxes aligned each placemat—some appropriate little gift, only for the ladies.

We loved to dance the Lindy; you were a great dancer. I always wanted to lead. You tried to teach me the steps of other dances, like the foxtrot, mambo, and samba. I didn't learn. I liked freestyle dancing. When we did our shimmy shake, we could clear the floor. I miss our dancing.

Other times, you would lecture me about the Vulture, that long-term relationship with a married man. You told me I was a disgrace. I remember that little speech in your office when we worked together. That speech may have been better suited for your daughter. But no, you treated her with kid gloves.

How could I ever forget the day I came over to your house to show you my beautiful two-and-a-half-carat engagement ring? I was so excited. It was my turn to be the bride. I just walked in when your daughter walked over and asked to see the ring. I gave it to her. I thought she wanted to try it on, but, no, she went into the bedroom. She came out with a jeweler's eyepiece to examine my ring. "Oh, you really got taken," she said. "How much did he pay for this? There's a big black speck in this ring."

As I put my ring back on, you said, "Well, she is a gemologist." This was news to me. When did she get her degree? She did work in a jewelry store and eventually became a manager. Apparently she felt her advanced position earned her an honorary gemology degree.

Why couldn't you just come out and say that Dolores the drunk was not supposed to marry a professional, educated, wealthy man who admired her? Clearly you felt that such an honor should be reserved for your daughter.

On my wedding day, you wrote such a beautiful note that I still have. You helped me pick out my wedding gown. You could show love, but then the Beast in you would come out.

After I was married and stopped working, the telephone would ring. I would pick up and your first remark would be, "Oh, did you just get up?" No matter what time of day it was, you always said that. I wanted to tell you, "Why, no, I've been awake for years." But you would never understand what "awake" truly meant.

After my mother died, I stayed in your basement. By then I was a full-blown alcoholic and drug addict. I suppose I should have been grateful I had a roof over my head. You complained about all my stuff and my sister's wedding gifts filling up the basement. I was ordered to get rid of things, but when I started sorting, some of the items found their way to the laundry room. How did they become yours when they couldn't be mine? Then there were my Britannica Encyclopedia books—one day I noticed the books were gone. Without asking me, you threw them away. Didn't you know that my father bought me those? They meant something to me, but suddenly they disappeared. What could I do?

The one good thing you did was insist that I see a doctor after I said I wanted to commit suicide. I didn't want to die, but I didn't know how to live. "You will not commit suicide here," you said. "Surely not on my watch." I saw a medical doctor first. He said I was depressed and sent me to a psychiatrist.

This was the start of my awakening and getting out of the basement. Where were you? What happened to the woman I knew? I got glimpses of that woman, but they grew further and further apart.

I'd been sober for three years when my car broke down. Without my knowledge, Middle Uncle asked you to donate $2,000 to my cause, so to speak. Middle Uncle's idea was for you, Father Uncle, and him each to put in $2,000 to help me get a new car with some money left for the dental work I needed. You said, "I don't take care of the checkbook—the Beast does." This was a downright lie. You paid all the bills and did the bank statements. You were the one who taught me how to balance a bank statement. Anyway, you seemed to think, "Why would Dolores need a new car when a used one would do?" And so you did not participate.

Come to think of it, you owed me money—money that I lent your daughter for a car. My darling mother said she would give your daughter $2,700 for a car. After my mother died, I lent your daughter the money. My great inheritance—$15,000—and I had to give you $2,700. Your daughter paid a small fraction of it back, maybe $200 or $300. Later, when I got sober, you paid me $300 for various things. There was still a significant remaining balance. Should I add interest? I considered it my rent.

Other times, you helped me with my clothing. At one time, we wore the same size and you gave me the clothes you didn't want. I took them, wore them, and was grateful. At birthdays, Christmas, and other occasions, you were a most generous person. There were fun times.

I told my husband about the Beast. He wondered why I kept going back to your house. He said, "You must be a saint." I told him I was no saint; I went back in search of the aunt I knew as a child. I still loved you, despite it all.

The saddest experience for me was when you had throat cancer. You had surgery to remove the cancer, and then four years later, it came back.

You were going for chemo and radiation treatments. I volunteered to take you on Tuesdays and Thursdays. It would be chemo in a doctor's office, followed by radiation. After each chemo session, you seemed to be in a fog. As we waited for your turn for radiation, you told me about the mask you had to wear over your face. You were as claustrophobic as I am. Though the radiation was brief, you couldn't wait to take off that mask.

Your name was called. You walked over to the radiation room. When I saw the red light above the door turn on, I knew you were getting the treatment, and I tried to imagine what it must be like.

One time, I heard the radiation technicians shouting your name, pleading with you to remain on the table with the mask. They shouted at you to please lie still as they recalibrated the machine. Something went wrong. You walked out of that room, shaky and angry. I held your arm to steady you as we walked to the car.

The last time I took you, you finished most of your radiation treatments. The doctor wanted to see you. You sat on that cold table with the white paper dangling on the floor. I stood to your right and the doctor to your left. He asked you to open your mouth so he could see your throat. You were moaning, but you opened your mouth painfully. As he looked, the doctor held your tongue down with a depressor. He talked as though you were in another room. "Oh," he said, "your throat is almost closed. You will need a feeding tube." Your eyes opened wide as you heard him speak. I couldn't believe my eyes as I looked into your mouth. There were so many sores. I tried to hold back the tears. I wanted to tell the doctor that the way he spoke to you was heartless. He said you would take two weeks off radiation and would need ten more treatments—for a total of thirty-three treatments

We left, and you never went back. I felt you made the right choice. The radiation would have killed you. Your skin turned a dark color from the treatment. You lost saliva and had to take medication for that. I'm sure you lived longer by stopping everything. In the end, cancer took your life.

My sister and I came to visit you. We walked into your bedroom. Your eyes were closed. Tubes were in you, and you had oxygen to help you breathe. My sister called out, "Aunt, I am here," but your eyes remained shut. On the other side of your hospital bed, I called, "Aunt, I am here," and said my name. When you heard my name, you opened your eyes. Our eyes met for that moment. That moment seemed to last a lifetime.

I saw suffering in your eyes. I say suffering because I knew your story. I knew your heartache. As our eyes locked, mine were saying good-bye to you for now, and, soon, on the other side, you would face the truth.

FATHER UNCLE

As THE TITLE suggests, you were my stand-in father. Every person in my life was "like a" (like a mother, like a father). Growing up, I waited for you to come home like a daughter waiting for her daddy.

You were so good to me. Your smile and the shine in your eyes told me I was special. You took me to see Santa Claus at Macy's in New York City. A picture shows me sitting on Santa's lap. When we passed a window where puppies were running through strips of newspaper, I asked you to get me a puppy. My dog, Tippy, had died, and I wanted another dog. You said you couldn't do that because Grandpa wouldn't like it.

After seeing Santa, we went to the toy store. Here I could pick whatever I wanted. I chose a walking doll.

Christmas was the most magical time of the year. The excitement started after Thanksgiving. There were many decorations to take down from the attic. I loved our big house with all the lights and outdoor decorations. We had candles, marching soldiers, carolers, Santa and his sleigh, and many lights. You were the perfectionist who put these up. I can still see you on the ladder with your staple gun.

You always chose very tall Christmas trees for the family. I remember the lights, beautiful ball ornaments, the Nativity scene under the tree with fake snow and villages, the big camel, the sheep, the shepherd, and the Wise Men—all in their place every year.

The tinsel that went on last was your forte. You placed it perfectly. Then you would lay a white fence that circled the tree.

We opened our presents on Christmas Eve after midnight Mass. So many gifts were under the Christmas tree. Most of them were for me. I always felt like the princess. You loved to surprise me. One year, I wanted a Schwinn three-speed bike.

You teased me and said I would be getting a lot of envelopes with money. You put an envelope opener near the tree. As we opened our presents, I didn't see the bike. I just assumed I didn't get it. After all the gifts were opened, I heard the creaking of the basement door. I turned, and you were bringing in the bike. It was white with black streamers, a horn, mirror, and bag carrier—fully loaded. As we hugged, I noticed you had tears in your eyes, tears of joy.

Another Christmas, you gave me a stuffed skunk. You told me to look closely at the skunk. There was a beautiful silver Wittnauer watch with diamonds.

Father Uncle, I remember how you liked to play the horses. It was late when you came home after going to the track. You were singing, "Cindy, oh Cindy, Cindy, didn't let me down." I don't know how much money you won. You gave me a hundred-dollar bill, which I promptly put in my savings account. Whatever money I received during the year, I saved. At Christmas, I used that money to buy gifts for everyone.

I would do anything for you. At dinnertime, I sat next to you. When Grandma made chicken soup, she would put liver in it. I disliked liver then, and I still do. You sometimes put liver in my dish and told me to eat it. Not wanting to disappoint you or lose your love, I gulped down the liver. You always laughed because you knew I did it for you. Feeling unwanted by my mother, I would do anything I thought was expected of me, whether I liked it or not.

Father Uncle, you also loved to bowl. When you came home from a bowling tournament, you always had something for me. While I loved the gifts, it meant so much that you thought enough of me to bring me a gift. I treasured not only your gifts, but gifts my other uncles brought. These were symbols of love, and I saved them. Some I still possess.

When I was a freshman in high school, I was sick with mononucleosis. I had to stay home the last semester of school. I had to pass algebra and biology Regents Exams in order to be promoted to sophomore year. A tutor came to the house to help me with biology. It was you, Father Uncle, who helped me with the algebra. I passed both courses and was promoted.

After Grandma died, you and Grandpa fought often. The year I graduated from high school, you left the house for good. You were carrying drawers full of your belongings to the car. I ran to see you. You said you had to go. You gave me a tin with pennies and silver dollars.

I cried as I watched you drive away. When I went back in the house, I saw a white envelope with my name on it placed on the staircase. It was my graduation card with a gift.

I didn't see much of you after that. You got married and had two children of your own. I cleaned out your desk drawer and found my dancing school program from Carnegie Hall. You had saved it.

When I did visit you, which wasn't too often, the feeling of our connection was gone. This felt like another rejection. The Father Uncle I knew died when you moved from the house. This new relative was someone I didn't know.

Years later, I went to visit you in the hospital. You were sick with cancer. All you said was, "Dolores, you put on weight." Was that all you could say? I was ready to answer you, but out of respect for you, I let that comment go. Where was the man I knew? Only a superficial person remained.

Occasionally, I visit your grave and put flowers on it. Did you hear what I said to you last time I visited? I thanked you for making me feel so special during my childhood. I choose to remember you that way.

FATHER

THE FIRST WORD that comes to my mind when I say the word *father* is *protector.*

I have no early recollection of you as my father. After I was born and lived with Grandma and the extended family, I hardly saw you.

You allowed Father Uncle to take over your role. I bonded with Father Uncle. Although I had a real father, you never came forward to claim your child.

This was very confusing. It was like the TV show "To Tell the Truth." Will my real father please stand up? I wanted you to stand up and find your voice, but you just let me go as if I never belonged to you.

When I was about five years old, I wanted to go to Cowboy City in New Jersey. You offered to take me. We never found Cowboy City, but we did find a Jersey fair. I remember touching a snake and a monkey's hand. When they asked who wanted to touch a snake, I volunteered and you said it was all right. We did have a good time together. We went home and the same pattern repeated. You isolated yourself upstairs, and I went downstairs to Grandma.

I often wondered why you spent so much time alone. Often you ate separately, cooking for yourself. I liked the macaroni and cheese you made and the kielbasa. You were 100 percent first-generation Czech. I remember the phrase you taught me, *Dej mi pusu,* which meant "Give me a kiss."

You would listen to my spelling words and help me with art projects. You were very good at painting, and you taught yourself to play the harmonica. I can still see and hear you playing "Have I Told You Lately That I Love You?" You liked country music.

Aunt told me that you would be drunk and your shoelaces would be untied when you picked up Mother for a date. How dare she talk about you like that? You weren't a beast.

You wanted to move to New Jersey and open a gas station with your friend. Mother told you she would not leave her mother's side. It was either the business or love. You chose love.

I never saw you drunk except at weddings or parties. You were a happy drunk. Alcohol really helped you let your guard down and have some fun. We would always dance the polka together. After the party, you would fall asleep. Those were the only occasions when you drank. I never smelled alcohol when I was around you.

You had the patience of a saint. Every Saturday, you would drive me and Grandma on our weekly shopping routine. First it was to Spinner's Food Market, and then the cold cut and bread store. Across the street at the general store, Grandma would get her oilcloth tablecloths, sugar bowls, and other household items. While we shopped, you would read your newspaper and drink coffee in the car.

At the cold cut store, Grandma and I would order a big hero sandwich. We shared it with you in the car on the way to the butcher shop. I always looked forward to Saturday with Grandma and you. Once we got home, you would go back to being alone.

You never took me to see Santa. Father Uncle took me. At Christmas, I never remembered gifts from you. All I remember was being showered with gifts and surprises from Father Uncle and other relatives. Somehow, despite all your neglect, I felt loved by you. You never put me down in any way.

I remember a time when I was about ten or eleven. My so-called friends left without me to go ice skating. I cried because I really wanted to go. I persuaded you to take me. You went ice skating with me. We both fell many times. After that, you would watch me skate.

I wanted you, Daddy. I wanted my real father. My real father. Why did you desert me? Why didn't you protect me from the Beast? I was your blood, wasn't I? I wanted you—not substitutes. Father Uncle later rejected me and broke my heart. He left me wondering what I had done to deserve this treatment.

I did everything that was asked of me. I knew what was expected, and I did it—because I wanted to be *loved*. To be loved and protected.

My high school was known for its afternoon tea parties. Mother never attended. She never participated in anything I did. But you—you did come with me to the Pop Hop every year.

Why didn't you stop the Beast? Grandma died, and the Beast rushed in with his comfort. The Beast became my friend before he came in for the kill. Didn't you know?

My "just like" relatives rejected me. I trusted no one. I trusted no one.

Father, how could you sleep? How could you, with even a doubt, let this go?

Your little girl, the Innocent Lamb, was robbed of everything. I was innocent. I was innocent, and nobody cared. Nobody!

Every little hope—every little dream—I had was gone. They were all taken from me. All this degradation was allowed to happen so easily.

Father, you supported me when I went to college. In fact, you even worked extra jobs so you could help me. You paid for my first year of college, and I took a loan for the other three years. You sent me so many caring cards and notes. I know because I saved them. Recently I found them. I read them and cried for that emotion you put into words.

If only—if only—but there is no "if only" in real life.

I remember when I went out with the Vulture. Mother told me you didn't want me to go with him. He was married and didn't treat me well. I never listened. I was well on my way to becoming a real alcoholic. I was ruined, and where were you? Still hiding—no voice, no voice.

For all those years we lived in the same house, you never spoke to me directly. I would wait for you to come home from work and ask you to take me to the diet doctor. You owned two cars. You left the "better one," at home, always driving the "problem car." Only you knew how to start it.

It is difficult to write about you without crying—without taking on the pain and loss of your death. I am always sorry for you. You were a good, honest man. My mind says, "Dolores, you know he *allowed* it." But my heart cries for you.

Please, God, help me get past crying—I have to let it go—he is in peace. So why can't I be at peace with all of this? There is so much damage that I have to examine. To go in-depth. To talk, to feel, to cry, to forgive, and heal.

It was so hard to see you working and working—working yourself to death. All this to satisfy Mother's endless demands. Her inner child was stamping her feet and saying, "I want. I want. I want!" You kept saying, "One day, I am going to keel over and die." It actually happened that way. I learned from this that thoughts and the words that are spoken out to the universe have more power than weapons of mass destruction. They most certainly do; I know this now.

It was a Monday morning, March 12, 1979. Did you know that most heart attacks occur on Mondays when people go back to work? My sister told me that she heard an inner voice say, "Go kiss your father good-bye; this is the last time you will see him." She didn't pay attention. She went back to sleep. You left early in the morning—the workhorse, the one who took care of everything.

Aunt picked me up, and we left for work. As soon as we arrived at the office, the phone rang, telling us to come home right away. Mother received a call from the police. Something had happened to Father. The Beast called us to pass on this news, but Aunt didn't tell me my father was dead. We got home. I was told that Father passed away on a subway platform. He was found on the platform—dead—and was taken to the morgue.

I didn't break down yet. The Beast would go to the morgue and identify the body. Wait, I insisted, I was going too. I had to see my father's face. I wondered if he suffered. Was his face distorted in any way? I had to know. I had to see for myself.

We left, the Beast complaining about the traffic for most of the way. Finally, we were standing outside the glass window. A blue curtain was pulled back. My father's mouth was open a little. I could see the space between his teeth where one was missing. His bridge was out of his mouth. The dark blue knit cap he always wore was still on his head. We identified the body, and the curtain was mercifully drawn.

We were asked a lot of questions. Was there foul play? No. Autopsy? No. The coroner said something about my father's chest. This man really worked. Did he ever take a vacation?

He is on vacation now, but I am still here.

The body was released to the funeral parlor, and we left. At that time, it all seemed so unreal. Mother was the one who was always sick.

Mother was in a state of shock. I could not hold the tears back—tears that went back to my birth.

After my grandmother died, my father would take my grandfather to visit Grandma's grave. My father would say that someday he would be buried by Henry's tombstone. He must have been psychic. There he lay, right near Henry. We didn't have our own cemetery plot. It was chosen for us.

I still see myself after the funeral at the dining room table. Food didn't comfort me, but the bottle did. I left the table and went into my bedroom with a bottle of J&B Scotch. I drank, crying for the daddy who never was. Finally, I passed out and went to sleep.

Sleep, Dolores, sleep, because the nightmare is by no means over. Sleep now—you will need all your strength to survive.

Daddy, why didn't you save me?

The Vulture: Long-Term Relationship with a Married Man

I CALL YOU the Vulture because this is the best description I can think of for you. Being with you was like being in a horror movie (what was it, about ten years?). I played the long, long reel over and over and over again—not only in therapy, but with every man I met. I am referring to men I met in recovery from alcoholism. Between you, Mother, and the Beast, I didn't have a chance from the start. I had no trust—especially in men.

I had a pet name for you—Muffin. Well, today you are a muffin, all right—a bran muffin. Today I shit you out-out-out-out of my system for good. How was a man like you ever allowed in my life? I would have to go back to my childhood (doesn't everything start there?). The lack of my real mother's love and her abandonment and the complete rejection of me as her child was my doorway to hell.

Every day you saw me walking to the subway on my way home from work. You owned a men's clothing shop across the street. You saw a beautiful young woman. It is hard for me to write *woman* here because I was nowhere near that. There I was, nicely clothed and presentable—except for one thing. A sign on my back read: easy prey, vulnerable, looking for love.

I don't know if it was the very first time you saw me that you ran across the street to introduce yourself. A successful businessman doesn't waste time—he goes for it.

I imagine a vulture circling and circling its prey. I saw your shadow, but I paid no attention to it. Each circle represents the times I refused to go out with you. My gut said no, but your persistence wore me down. I didn't know then how dead my spirit was, but negative energy was flowing from my being. An aura of darkness surrounded me. I was unaware of what easy prey I was.

As you, the Vulture, circled and circled and came down for your meal, I was knocked off my feet. I allowed you to devour me—yes, devour me—my body, mind, and spirit.

As I felt those claws grab my midsection, forcing me to lie still, I shouted, "Thank you, Mommy!"

As the Wizard approached the Vulture, she saw how self-absorbed he was. He was narcissistic to the core.

The Vulture crossed and uncrossed his legs several times. He glanced around the room, looking for a clock. There were no keepers of time in the Hall of Recollection.

Having to participate in this hearing was a waste of time to him. There were trips, deals, and money to be made. He didn't want to hear. If he couldn't hear, how could he listen? The Wizard proceeded to speak. It was important to address him whether he listened or not. This was for her.

I could never figure out why I was so attracted to you. You were twenty-three years older than I was, of slight build with blue eyes. It wasn't until I got sober and went to therapy that I realized you were brother to the Beast. Not by blood—it was my subconscious that held me to you. You were the image of the Beast in my mind. This image remained fixed until I sought help. Abuse was familiar to me.

From the very start, you made those married-man promises. I called this the married-man's lament. You were in the process of leaving your wife, getting your own apartment and then the divorce. You were in the process for how many years? Maybe you still are in the process.

I fell time and time again for your lies. You knew my weaknesses so well. I wanted to be taken care of because I never felt capable of taking care of myself.

When I met you, I was a daily drinker and used speed. I was in my midtwenties. A great isolator, on weekends, I would spend my time sitting in a rocking chair with earphones, listening to music, drinking amaretto, and smoking joints. This helped me get out of my unbear-able life into my dream of what I wanted my life to be.

I was afraid of men. The attention I received frightened me. I didn't know how to handle it, and I felt they wanted me for only one reason—sex. I stayed away from men. There were some affairs with married men, but those all ended when I wanted to be taken seriously. Then I met you.

When I think about it now, I can't believe the years of misery I went through, listening to your lies. There came a point when I would do anything for you. Anything you wanted I would do because I wanted to be loved and taken care of.

I had been scarred so deeply from the abandonment of my mother. I didn't know how damaged I was by the Beast and the Last Secret. But you saw my weaknesses, and you used me knowing my weaknesses. That's what hurts the most.

I put all my faith in you to change my life. My drinking escalated to the point where blackouts became an occurrence every time I drank.

You brought me to places I never knew existed. I was a good Catholic schoolgirl with no education about the world you exposed me to.

You took me to a swinging club. To me it was a modern-day Sodom and Gomorrah.

Walking in, I saw a dance floor. I proceeded to the locker room with other women changing into their sexy lingerie.

A swimming pool and private rooms were available for whatever. The most unbelievable scene was at the back of the place. I saw many mats (like exercise mats) scattered throughout the huge room. On top of those mats, people were fucking in all different positions. That smell of sweat and semen gave an intense odor to the room.

If I hadn't experienced it, I could not imagine this. For people who indulge in swinging and want to do this, I have no objection. I didn't want to be there, yet I was there and I participated.

You introduced me to swinging. You told me we were going to your friend's house for dinner. When I got there, it was a swinging party. Everyone loosened up after smoking a few joints and drinking. We proceeded to go downstairs. There was a hot tub. Another room held sex toys and beautiful stained-glass etchings of various sexual positions. When I got drunk enough, I was your puppet and I would do anything you wanted.

After the initial sexual frenzy, we would go upstairs and partake of the lavish dishes of food displayed on the dining room table. These parties would last into the early morning. Then you would take me home.

For the more advanced swinging parties, there was the time when you told me we were going away for the weekend. When we had driven upstate and I got out of the car, I noticed familiar faces. They were part of the swinging scene. On that weekend, the place was closed for swinging only. In fact, it was called the Swinging Fantasy Weekend.

People were fulfilling their sexual fantasies. My fantasy was to find a man who loved me to whom I could give my love to in a committed relationship. I thought this would never be a part of my life.

I drank more and more because the reality of my life, the loneliness, was too painful. I never drank for fun—I drank to escape.

My life kept escalating downward. The terrible events included my father dying suddenly. The house was about to go into foreclosure. Luckily a buyer appeared. My sister got married and moved out of the country. My mother and I moved into Aunt's basement. Two months later, my mother died. Now I crossed over to being a real alcoholic. *The Big Book of Alcoholic Anonymous* says, "The real alcoholic has a physical allergy and there is no human defense against the first drink." There came a point in my drinking where alcohol was no longer my friend. It didn't take away the pain. I could not stop drinking no matter what.

I was living in the basement (or should I say, staying in the basement), desperately wanting to be on my own—away from the Beast, away from you, who told me I was living in a hovel.

I started going to a club that was on the water not far from where I lived. I thought it was very classy. It had valet parking and a multilevel dance floor. What I loved the most was the bar. It was circular and very clean.

It would take me hours to get prepared. My clothes were just so, and I was really high on speed and alcohol before I left. The first time at the club, I ordered my drink of choice—a Black Russian. Taking it from the bar, my hand shook. It shook because I was so nervous in the crowd. The loneliness would overtake me, and I had to get out. I had to be with people—no matter what happened.

Most of the time, I would go into a blackout and leave with someone. The next morning, I was unaware of where I was and what had happened. One morning, I awoke in Brooklyn. The man, a recent jailbird, told me that if he hadn't grabbed the steering wheel of the car, I would've driven off the bridge. This didn't scare me enough to stop drinking.

A real alcoholic is never scared by a doctor's warning, a family's speeches, or driving with children in the car. This disease—and it is a disease—takes hold of one's body, mind, and soul. There is nothing in life for a real alcoholic except getting the booze. Promises are made that are meant to be kept at that moment. They never can be because of the compulsion that is set in motion once alcohol touches one's lips. So many times I wanted to stop. In the morning, I would promise myself I would not drink. By eleven o'clock, that thirst was there—the thirst that only alcohol could quench. So it would be another drinking day.

You, the Vulture, never tried to help me in any way. You told me to look for an engagement ring. I was so excited that I started looking. Then you took back your word. Of course, after that I wouldn't see you for a while.

Finally, I took a huge step and left the basement. I found a beautiful summer rental apartment on the beach. What a difference to wake up to the sun and see the birds leaving their little footprints on the sand every morning. I loved to listen to the surf pounding at night. I was told it was foolish to spend $6,000 for the summer rental, but it was paradise for me. I didn't have a job; my money was running out from my inheritance, but it didn't matter.

I had another blackout experience. A man invited me to his apartment, and I followed him in my car. I walked into his apartment and saw an ironing board with an iron on top of it. Then I blacked out. I woke up in the morning between two men. I tried not to wake them while I got dressed to leave. They woke up. They started speaking in Arabic. As I proceeded to leave, one of them put his arm up against the door to prevent me from leaving. At the time, Porsche sunglasses were very popular. He saw mine and said I was stealing his. When I pointed to his pair on the dresser, he let me go. As I walked to my car, I swore I would never go to the club again. Every time I went there, I would wind up in places like this. Such was my DENIAL, (Don't Even Know I Am Lying). It never crossed my mind that it was the booze and not the place that was my problem.

The summer was coming to an end. You didn't help me find a new place. You never put your hands in your pocket for anything unless it would serve your purpose. Middle Uncle's wife came to me and said I could live with them and they would help me start a new life—if I stopped seeing you, the Vulture. I agreed. I told you I did not want to see you again. I moved out of state, and I was glad to be rid of you. I sincerely wanted to make a new start. But like all geographical cures, I took myself with me. I drank secretly.

Just before Christmas, we spent the day decorating the tree. Afterward, everyone was relaxing in the den. I was going back and forth into my room. Middle Uncle's wife followed me and saw me take the bottle of scotch from the closet and drink from the bottle. She went into a rage, hit me, pulled my hair, and jumped on my most precious stereo. No one had ever hit me before—I was so frightened. There is no delicate way to put this: I shit in my pants.

If I had cancer, I would have been hugged.

As I went upstairs to take a shower, a family conference was taking place. I was told I could stay if I went to AA. I agreed. The next day, I spoke to one of Middle Uncle's friends who was in AA. He told me I had a disease that was not my fault and I was a good person. I felt so relieved to hear that it was a disease and I could do something about it.

On December 16, 1982, two ladies in recovery arrived. They took me to my first AA meeting. One of the ladies purchased *The Big Book of Alcoholics Anonymous* for me. On the inside cover, she wrote the date, December 16, 1982, and "Dear Dolores, Welcome to a new life. Love, Kathy."

I didn't remember too much about the first meeting—only that they said that it was the first drink that got you drunk. What really impressed me was that *I* was putting the booze into my body.

Middle Uncle—who loved me very much—asked me that if I couldn't stay sober for myself, to stay sober for him. I tried to keep my promise.

It wasn't easy for me to live under other people's rules. You can't just tell an alcoholic not to drink and they won't drink. The sleepless nights and the pains in my stomach were something I could not share with anyone.

Then I got a job at a brokerage house with the help of Middle Uncle. Could you imagine I was working in the margin department of a brokerage firm? Part of my job was doing research. I would have to make a copy of a small negative that fit into a very small slot in a machine. Trying to fit the negative into the small slot when you have the shakes was impossible. I would hold my right wrist with my left hand, but it didn't work. I was very embarrassed when I had to ask someone else to do it for me. I needed a drink to calm me. That afternoon at lunchtime, I had Black Russians—one after another—until the shakes subsided.

I never stole money to pay for drinking or drugging. I stole other people's peace of mind. As a blackout drinker, there was no telling what I'd do.

When Middle Uncle asked me if I was drinking, I said no. I knew they would throw me out. I knew they would keep their word and I would have to leave. They meant business. I wanted to tell him that I needed to go to a rehabilitation center, but I kept everything locked inside. I was too afraid to speak about it.

At this point, my sister and her husband returned home. She was living at her mother-in-law's house. I spent time there, and I wanted to find my own place. They helped me, and I found an apartment on the water. When you live in a beach town, you must live on the beach. That's my philosophy. I could afford it with the little money I made. I moved into my new place.

I had very little furniture. I didn't have a TV or a table on which to eat. None of this mattered because I was on my own. When Middle Uncle and his wife came to my apartment, they brought in a new stereo system. They helped me decorate my apartment with drapes, a TV, and a kitchen table with four chairs. They brought bags of food and household products. Aside from that terrible night, they were very caring to me. Many years later, Middle Uncle told me that he wanted to cry when he left. He wanted a better place for me to live. This was my starting place.

I was still drinking. One Friday night I walked into my apartment. Loneliness became my best friend. I drank to go into a blackout. I looked at myself in the mirror. I held up the glass and remembered what they said at AA: I was pouring the drink into me. It wasn't my mother, the Beast, or the Vulture. It was me. That was a Friday night, and I woke up Sunday afternoon. A three-day blackout had never happened to me before. It scared me. I knew that if I continued drinking, I would lose my job and my apartment. Then where would I be? I went to some AA meetings and listened, but I never connected. After that, I used my willpower to stay off booze for three months. Every cell of my body called for booze.

On the afternoon of September 15, some of my coworkers took me to lunch for my birthday. It was a very hot day. I was wearing a white skirt below the knee with buttons going down the middle, a black polo shirt, and a white cap-sleeve sport jacket. My black strap high heels pounded the pavement with each step. I was salivating for a drink. My brain and every part of me wanted to drink. I wondered if other people around me could see this madness in my eyes. I managed not to drink at the luncheon.

You were taking me out to dinner that night. We went to a restaurant that we visited frequently. We sat down to dinner across from each other. You said, "You have not been drinking. Let me order you a Black Russian." I said OK. This was my drink of choice. The waitress placed the Black Russian before me, and I looked at it with a tortured soul. I wanted it so desperately. I picked it up, put the glass to my mouth, took a sip—a very small sip—and felt my temples beating in my forehead. I could feel that familiar heat going down my throat and throughout my body. I put the drink down. I went to the ladies room and knelt down on the floor. I asked God to help me as I didn't want to drink. I was willing to do anything to stop. As I left the ladies room, the compulsion, that overriding thirst, left me. After that moment, I never drank again. That was 1983.

I went to AA. I started working the twelve-step program. At the meeting I saw a can of Goya beans on the podium. I wondered if that was the cure. After the meeting, I asked about the can of Goya beans. The woman laughed and told me GOYA meant "Get Off Your Ass." I would learn that AA is a program of action.

In AA, suggestions were given. Whether I accepted these suggestions was up to me. If I had been told what to do, I would have walked out the door.

I felt at home at the meeting. I wanted to live without drugs, alcohol, and unhealthy relationships. I wanted to know me without being anesthetized. Once I entered the doors of AA, my suffering was over. Suffering was optional. There would be pain, but there would also be joy. My suffering was over because for the first time I was aware.

What amazed me most was that when I went back to the meeting the following week, people remembered what I had said. They asked me how I was doing. I wasn't criticized or judged. For the first time in my life, I felt accepted. Listening to other people's struggles in life without drinking encouraged me that I could do the same. There were so many things I wanted: a better place to live, a better job, a good relationship with a man. I realized that these things would take TIME ("Things I Must Earn").

I thought that once I stopped drinking, everything would be great. I needed more than the AA program to recover. I went to the alcohol treatment center. I didn't have the insurance or the funds to go to a private therapist. Here I could pay what I could afford. The people I saw were earning their degrees in psychology. I got what I needed. When I was working, I paid five dollars a week for therapy. Between jobs, they asked for two dollars a week. I was very grateful for the people who listened to me through my tears. They encouraged me to talk about my feelings. This was very difficult for me. It was hard for me to trust anyone.

I was on cloud nine. Every day that I did not drink or drug, I was a winner. I had never felt like a winner. Everything I learned about living, I learned from the program.

In the beginning, I mouthed, "I am an alcoholic." It took a while before I believed that with my heart. I kept going to meetings and listening to people's stories. I knew I was an alcoholic. I knew that I could not ingest alcohol or drugs.

My life consisted of going to work, coming home, eating something, and going to a meeting. I did this every day. Before long, I had my thirty-day coin. I felt a sense of accomplishment. These people were just like me. I related to them. No matter what I said or how distorted it sounded, they understood my thinking.

I had friends—friends who would not leave me behind. Friday nights, after the meeting, we would go to the diner. They would set up the table and chairs for about twenty people. We would stay and talk until the early morning. There were no longer any lonely Friday nights.

There were so many things to do in AA, but group anniversaries were my favorite. The first one I went to was held in a big auditorium. There was dancing, food, and prizes. I had a great time. I looked around the room and saw so many people having a good time, smiling and dancing without the use of alcohol or drugs.

At my job, things were not going too well. My supervisor complained about how slow I was. I wasn't working fast enough. Did she know that I was detoxing from alcohol and speed? My first priority was staying sober. Without my sobriety, I had nothing. I was transferred from department to department.

One afternoon, as I was sitting at my desk, a man holding an envelope came toward me. It was from Middle Uncle. I opened the envelope, and there was a hundred-dollar bill in it. The note said, "We are very proud of you." I had reached my three-month sobriety, my ninety days.

Getting up at 6:15 in the morning and having to make the 7:10 train to Penn Station was quite a chore for me. From the age of sixteen, I used speed every day to get me out of bed. Now, I was always late. I really didn't want to work in the city anymore. The daily commute entailed driving to the station, taking the Long Island Rail Road to the city, taking the subway, and walking to the office.

In AA, the old-timers (those who have long-term sobriety) said that drinking was no longer an option. If drinking was no longer an option, what would I put in place of it? When the thought of taking a drink entered my mind, I would make a phone call to someone in AA, go to a meeting, or read some of the literature. I was taught in AA to "think the drink through" and where it would take me—back to the insanity of drinking.

Just because I was in recovery didn't mean that I didn't think of a drink. Being alcoholic, my natural state was to drink. Whether it's genetic or I lack dopamine or serotonin in my brain, I do not try to figure it out anymore. I accept that I am an alcoholic and take responsibility for my sobriety. When I was unaware, I was accountable—not responsible. Now that I am aware, I am responsible.

When I was in my ninth month of sobriety, I was called into the supervisor's office where I worked. I was told to leave. Previously, they had given me a warning about getting more work done. Now, I was fired.

As I left the World Trade Center on this beautiful summer day, I was happy. It was a great relief to be out of that atmosphere. I vowed I would get a job on Long Island.

I applied for unemployment, but I was told that my old company was denying my unemployment benefits. They said that I had been given a warning so they did not have to pay me anything. When I heard this, FEAR ("False Evidence Appearing Real") took over me. I started to project. Whenever I projected into the future, it was always negative. I am always the loser. I saw myself losing my apartment, but the worst thing that happened was that the compulsion to drink was back in full force. I could actually taste the alcohol. I started smoking cigarettes. I had given them up before so I knew I could do it again, but I smoked to get through this hurdle.

I read the *Daily Word*. Middle Uncle's wife purchased a subscription for me. It was a monthly booklet that was sent out by Unity. There was a message for each day of the month. On the back of the cover was a phone number for a minister. The day before I had to go in front of the unemployment board, I called Unity. I spoke to the minister about the upcoming meeting and how frightened I was. He told me to go to the meeting and tell the truth. He said everything would be OK. We prayed together.

When I went to the meeting, I was very nervous. Since I had worked at my job for more than a year, there was no way they could deny me my unemployment benefits. I was so relieved when it was over—and I was so grateful that I didn't drink over something like that.

It took another week before I received an unemployment check. My checking account had less than thirty dollars. I lived from week to week. A surprise check came in the mail. It was my pension money from the brokerage firm. I found that every time I needed something, it was provided. I knew that my Higher Power would see me through. I didn't have everything I wanted, but I had what I needed.

One of the things that really bothered me in my apartment was that there was no light fixture in the kitchen. It was just a light bulb. I felt sorry for myself that I couldn't buy a fixture. In the program I heard that my circumstances might remain the same, but my attitude toward those circumstances would change. When I went home that night, I looked at that bulb differently. I saw the perfect form and the perfect function of Thomas Edison's efforts. I looked at it as a work of art and genius. I thought of Andy Warhol and the Campbell's Soup can. The light bulb was perfect just the way it was. I never thought about getting a fixture after that.

I began looking at things differently. I stopped feeling sorry for myself. I loved being responsible for myself. I loved living on my own and making my own choices. I didn't want to give that power away. The best thing was that I didn't have to as long as I stayed sober. No one could hurt me or touch me in any way unless I gave them my permission.

I did have a few small roaches in my apartment. Just knowing they were there made me very cautious around the sink, taking a shower, or when I walked into the apartment. I would open the door and say, "I'm home, critters." I'd turn on the light before I walked in and hope there were none to be seen. I laughed at myself that I never wanted to wash dishes at the sink because of them. I called my sister, who was living at her mother-in-law's house nearby, and asked if I could bring over some dishes to put into the dishwasher. I placed my dirty dishes in a suitcase with a towel to keep them from breaking and went over to use the dishwasher.

There was an old refrigerator. It was one of those with ice that needed to be defrosted. Well, I never got around to it. Nature took care of it for me. There was a storm, and the electricity went out. The roof was taken off one of the buildings behind mine, but nothing happened to my building. When I walked into my kitchen, there was a flood on the floor. The refrigerator was defrosted, and I laughed.

My unemployment was coming to an end and so was the summer. It was time to look for a job. This was a new experience for me. Middle Uncle had always helped me with jobs. Now I had to do it for myself.

I was terrified of picking up the phone and calling employment agencies. Pacing back and forth in the kitchen, I looked at the telephone on the table. This was part of growing up.

As I paced, I talked to myself. *I'm just calling another human being. You say you want to be on your own, so now you must make the call. Make the call.* I called an employment agency. The man who answered was in charge. I told him my previous work experience. He had a client looking for someone with my abilities. She operated a business from her home. It was located about twenty minutes from my apartment.

The next day, he called. She was interested. An interview was set up. We hit it off immediately. She said that she wanted to interview me because we went to the same high school. She hired me, and I began working the next day. I made a little less money at this job, but I did not have to travel to the city. I was grateful for that.

During my first year of sobriety, I felt the need to go to confession and talk to a priest. I told him the truth about everything, except the last secret. At that time, I wasn't ready to talk about the last secret. When I finished, he said, "You have no penance; you have suffered enough." I left the confessional with tears in my eyes.

Just before my first anniversary, I experienced my first drunk dream. It was frightening. The dream seemed so real. Drunken dreams are a common occurrence. In some of them, I drank. In others, I stated I was an alcoholic and could not drink. When I woke up from these dreams, I wondered if I was in a blackout. Usually just before my AA anniversary, my sleep was interrupted by a drunk dream.

I was so excited for my first AA anniversary. In AA, an anniversary was a big celebration. There were balloons, banners, and a cake. Family members and friends were invited. It was an example that the program worked.

My birthday and my anniversary are on the same day. This was very fitting, as I felt I had a new birth when I entered the rooms of AA. The room was filled with group members and my family. I was called up to the podium to give a few words. My heart was full of gratitude to everyone who had helped me to get to this place. I did not do it alone. I thought back to when I had seen the Goya can on the same podium. After the meeting, a party had been prepared for me by my relatives and friends. It was overwhelming.

The real work began during my second year of sobriety. In addition to meetings, I went to therapy. I volunteered to speak at meetings. I remember being up on stage and just crying. I was crying about the abuse. I spoke and cried. The room was silent. When I finished, I thought back—I didn't even mention drinking. Members hugged and assured me that I would get better and this was all part of the process.

I promised myself that I would give up smoking in my second year of sobriety. The lady I worked for and I were chain smokers. My motivation to stop smoking was not my health. With the money I made, I could not have my hair done and a manicure once a week if I smoked. So smoking would have to go.

At first, I went to Smoke Enders at the hospital. I took a lot of the suggestions, such as putting the butts into a can and smelling them.

They advised cutting back on cigarettes. By this time, I was up to four packs a day. I was never one for cutting back. It was all or nothing for me. If I possessed cigarettes, I was going to smoke them.

I did some research about what happens in the brain when one stops smoking. Every time I did not smoke a cigarette, I was cutting the connections between the synapses in the brain—those tiny strands that reach to other cells. Those connections had to be broken. I prepared myself for a foggy state of mind. I set up a date to start. I took a jar to work with me. For every hour that I did not smoke, I put a penny in the jar. As I saw the pennies accumulate, I did not want to go back on my word and smoke a cigarette. The lady I worked with was amazed at my willpower. I gained weight, but I stopped smoking. It was all part of withdrawal. Since 1984, I have not smoked a cigarette.

I have always been interested in different religions and different beliefs and pathways to God. I started going to church with my friend Angela. I think it was a born-again Christian church. One night, a minister from out of state led the service. He said, "There is one among us that has a great financial need." He pointed to me and called me to the front of the congregation. He asked me what was wrong. I started to cry as I told him about you, the Vulture. I wanted you out of my life. The minister looked at me and said, "You must get that man out of your life, and the gates of heaven will be open to you." He called the congregation up to the front of the room. They formed a circle around me, held their hands over me, and prayed for me. After the service, people came up to me and asked what I needed.

It took a little longer and a lot more pain before I could completely rid myself of you. I was in my third year of sobriety. My apartment was going to be demolished to build new condos. I had three months to find a new place to live. Without a job, living on unemployment, I was beside myself. You offered your studio apartment for me to live in. You continued going on and on about me moving into your studio apartment. You didn't know that if you didn't come through for me now, I vowed never to see you again. This was it—and I meant it. I had an alternate plan for moving. My friends in the program and my sister helped me move.

My sister was living in a nearby apartment. She told me I could stay with her. Her husband was going into the military, and she would join him in three months. The day I moved, you never showed up. This was no surprise to me. I went to Mass at the Catholic Church near my apartment. During the sermon I heard the priest say, "Put your trust in God, and He will help you." Those words stuck with me. I came home, and I wrote them down on a piece of paper. I committed everything to God. I sought help from God. I moved in with my sister, and I put the note next to the telephone. You called repeatedly. With each call, I read the note and hung up the phone. *I will not allow you back in my life. I will never go back to you.*

I was frozen with fear having to find a new job. My sister would wake me up in the morning and tell me to get busy, as she would be moving soon. I called a friend in the program, and we searched for jobs together. I got a job interview. They called me back for three interviews. I had to borrow clothes so I could have three different outfits. They didn't hire me. Then there was a job interview on the North Shore. They interviewed me, and I got the job that day. It was a full-time bookkeeping position that paid me more money than I had ever made. I was so happy to have a job.

On the way home, a young man in front of me stopped short and I hit his bumper. I pulled over to the side, and I offered to pay for the damages. The spoiler on his car was damaged. After I paid him, I had very little money left. I was still living with my sister for the first few weeks of my new job.

I had to find a new place to live. Most of the places I could afford were garage apartments. I decided to let people know I needed a place to live. I was taught to let people know where I was coming from and to ask for help. A lady where I worked came to me and said that she was renting her basement apartment. It was very close to my job. I went to see it. There were steep steps going down and a small kitchen, and everything was one big, open space. It was clean, but it did have a slight smell of a basement. I didn't have a stove, but that didn't matter. I'd use a hot plate. It was a very low price, and she did not ask me for a security deposit. I felt that my Higher Power was directing me, as I did not have the money for a security deposit. It afforded me extra money to be able to do some nice things for myself. I was happy. Friends helped me move into my new place.

My sobriety became sacred to me. It represented the hub of a wheel, and each spoke represented my relationships with God, my family, my job, and whatever I was doing in my life. Without sobriety, there would be no life.

If medical research developed a pill that I could take on a daily basis to stop drinking, I would not take it. For me, there was a difference between not drinking and sobriety. Putting the cork in the bottle was the first step. Changing the person who had brought me to this point was the real work. As the saying goes—half measures availed us nothing.

When I read the statistics about who would make it and who would not, I wanted to laugh. There were no statistics in A.A. There was a missing variable in the equation that no one could determine. That was the spiritual connection that no one could measure.

I knew a man who had long-term sobriety. He used to panhandle for nickels and dimes and live on the street. On a very cold night, he decided to go into the church basement where an AA meeting was taking place. His intention was to get warm and have a cup of coffee. As he entered the room, there was a greeter at the door. Despite his disheveled appearance and dirty hands, the greeter shook his hand and welcomed him. This was his turning point to stop drinking. It was the first time in a long time that he felt like human being.

I was just about to leave for work when the telephone rang. It was you, the Vulture. You asked if you could take me out for dinner. It was as if nothing had ever happened. I hung up and went to work. I called the telephone company, and I told the woman I was being stalked by an old boyfriend. She gave me an unlisted number. I didn't have to pay for it. Everything that the minister talked about was coming to fruition because I got rid of you.

Still, Vulture, you never stopped. You had the telephone number of friend of mine. You constantly called her to find out about me. Was I still sober? Did I get married? Did I have children?

The last time you spoke to my friend, you told her you had Parkinson's disease. You needed to talk to me. Why? Were you going to make amends to me?

You fooled me so many times that I never believed you. For example, when I lived at Middle Uncle's, you sent me divorce papers. They looked authentic. They were probably drawn up by one of your lawyer friends.

How about when you presented me with a ring? It was not an engagement ring. You said it was a diamond. I looked at it, and I knew it wasn't a diamond. Yet, you insisted. I doubted myself and took the ring to a jewelry store. The jeweler told me it was a glass ring. I was not shocked by this. What shocked me was that I continued to see you.

When you offered to buy me a fur jacket, we went to a fur salon. I picked out a jacket. Then you changed your mind. It cost too much. Yet, you were a multimillionaire. I was dirt cheap. That night, I cried, "This is not love. I am sober now—I told you to stay out of my life." What did you do? You came to my apartment and knocked and knocked on the door. I told you to go away. I never wanted to see you again. You pretended you had the fur jacket and left a box on the steps. Yeah, sure. It was London Fog raincoat with detachable lining. I wore it as a winter coat.

You saw that I slept with an electric heater on a small table near my head. In the winter, there was hardly any heat. The wind went through the apartment as if the walls were made of paper. Still, you didn't care. You always showed up. You knew where I lived. I really needed a court order of protection to keep you away from me.

I did see you once in Montauk. I was happily married. My husband and I were going to have lunch at a restaurant on Fisherman's Wharf. As I glanced out the window, I saw you. You were in your nautical outfit (all white with your captain's hat on). There you were in all your splendor. You were laughing with two of your friends. It was outside my favorite clothing store in Montauk, Summer Stock. I was glad we never came face-to-face.

You taught me a great lesson. You taught me what love is not.

The Woman Who Happened to be a Nun

How COULD I ever forget you? You were my first grade teacher—my first experience in school. I never went to kindergarten. My home life consisted of adults. In other words, I was very shy—very shy. Do you get it now? Did you know I threw up almost every morning before going to school?

Sometimes, as I walked to school, Aunt and Middle Uncle would accompany me. At one point, they would cross the street to go to the subway. As they crossed, they would look back and wave to me. My heart sank, my stomach tightened, and there was sweat on brow—I did not want to face that nun again.

As I sat at my desk with folded hands, you stood at the blackboard with that pointer stick. You were old and ready for retirement, frighteningly tall to an Innocent Lamb.

When you called someone to give an answer, that child had to stand up at the side of the desk. When you called on me, I never responded—although I knew the answers. I wasn't stupid. I was afraid to speak. You insisted I was stupid. With my bowed head and feeling embarrassed, I sat down. You never let up picking on me—yes, picking on me. Don't deny it. My mother was called for a conference. What did you question her on—my stupidity? No, you asked why she didn't have more children. This was none of your business.

You branded me stupid. Besides being a fatso, stupid was another label added to my back. Little did I know that the Innocent Lamb possessed a winning spirit, and in her silent voice, she said, "I'll show you who's stupid."

When I went back to school the following year, you were retired. I hoped I'd never see you again. But your voice saying *stupid, stupid* never left my ears.

THE MAN WHO HAPPENED TO BE A PRIEST

How COULD YOU call yourself a priest? A priest is an instrument of Christ on earth, forgiving and compassionate. At least, that's what I thought before going to confession. In Catholic school, we attended Mass as a group. After my deflowering by the Beast, I would not go to Communion. Of course, the nuns noticed. One must go to confession and Communion.

I decided to take a chance and go to confession. Maybe I could reveal the secret to you, a representative of Christ. I'd try. This secret was so hard to carry. When I entered the confessional, I was very anxious. As the little box slid open for me to speak, I said, "Bless me, Father, for I have sinned. It has been two months since my last confession." I didn't waste any time. But could I tell him who the Beast was? No! I disguised the Beast as a married man that I was having sex with. "What, you tramp! Yes, exactly, tramp; and for your penance say five rosaries." I wondered if I was forgiven. You didn't say.

You knew I was a student. Did you bother to inquire and dig deeper? Or did you pass judgment on me? Was it something from your past that you couldn't face that brought so much rage out of you? I never said the five rosaries, and I didn't go back to confession until 1983. The nuns were fine as long as I went up to Communion and stuck out my tongue to receive the Host. Only now I had another label to carry: tramp.

I will not protect my abusers anymore.
All secrets must be brought out to the light.
I will not punish myself.
I will not punish myself.
I will not punish myself.
I will not punish myself.
I will not punish myself
For things I did not do.

THE LAST SECRET

I REMEMBER YOUR mother when she was pregnant with you. At some point in her pregnancy, an unexpected surge of bleeding began. She had to stay in bed for the rest of her pregnancy or she could lose you.

Your mother and sister stayed with us. My mother did all the work of cooking and cleaning. I watched your sister. I felt like the older sister. Everything went fine. You were a healthy baby.

I guess you don't remember when you fell down the basement steps. You were two or three years old. You slipped and came tumbling down the steps. I saw you and quickly put out my hand. I managed to grasp your head and prevented you from having a bad injury. You came down head first.

You asked me to be your sponsor at confirmation. You tried to teach me to drive a stick shift with that car. I never learned.

I wonder how it got to where it did. When we saw each other, I always wondered if you ever thought about our past. I did!

I remember sitting in the living room on the orange chair from Grandma's house. I was waiting for my pot delivery. You came in and bent over and kissed me on the mouth. You left right away, out the back door. I do not remember our first sexual encounter.

I remember you sleeping in my room. Only we weren't sleeping—we were fucking.

I felt guilty because I was older than you. Did I hurt you and ruin your life as the Beast did to me? Was I to blame for that? I dared not look at it at the time. Even when I got sober and went to therapy, I wasn't ready to take it apart, for this was something I could not share then.

I felt very uncomfortable about you. Actually, I never opened up to it until very recently. Look how long I kept this last secret! I wanted to leave you out of this book, but you were a dark secret that deeply affected me and my life. A friend said, "Why are you protecting someone who hurt you, an abuser, a part of the Beast?"

To be honest, holding this secret was more for my sake than for yours. I still didn't want anyone to know. Ultimately, this dark secret made me sick because it hurt me, affecting my self-esteem. It had to be revealed. I did talk about it to my psychiatrist as I talked about my feelings of guilt toward you. He said I was already ruined by the Beast. When the Beast made up those names about me, you thought they were funny too. Can you feel it? I was already ruined! After my mother died—a year after my father—I never understood how you could be so cruel.

I remember sitting in the living room in your house. You asked your mother, "How long is she going to stay here?" At the time, I thought you didn't realize I could hear you. Now I think it didn't matter if I heard or not. Didn't you know how hurt I felt?

Did you think I wanted to stay in a basement? Especially that basement, where at any time, you or the Beast could drop in on me? My legs—especially my calves—ached from standing on a cement floor. Your sister often left the basement door open while she ironed in the morning. Since I left for work before her, I would ask, "Please close the basement door when you leave because the dog comes down and pees on my bed, jumps on the table, knocks over and breaks everything." He destroyed my plant—the one living thing I had in the basement. Did she listen? Sometimes, but mostly not.

I would have gladly granted your wish to leave your house forever. You could have your basement and use it to set up whatever you wanted.

When I did move out of your basement, you stayed in your room with your girlfriend. My sister and brother-in-law helped me pack my things. This was the end of sex with you and the Beast. I was thirty-one.

Who would think my life would be so affected by this last secret? I was ashamed and always felt guilt about it. It took years for me to bring it out of the closet of my mind. Over the years, I read many self-help books. They taught me that keeping secrets makes you sick. As they say, "You are as sick as your secrets."

Having released this last secret, I am freed from the negative energy that kept me from the manifestation of my dreams. Yes, my dreams. I have dreams.

Once the last perpetrator was addressed, they returned to the Chamber. Here they were given a choice. They could go to the House of Mirrors or the Mansion of Truth and Jubilation.

Without hesitation, the Beast and the Vulture decided to go to the House of Mirrors. The others wished to go to the Mansion of Truth and Jubilation.

THE HOUSE OF MIRRORS

A GUIDE BROUGHT the Vulture and the Beast along a windy dirt road. It was a long walk. Then there was a clearing. There was so much darkness. The house was invisible to them. The guide assisted them to the front door. Once opened, there was much illumination from all the mirrors. There were many people sitting cross-legged (yogi style) on tremendous cushions.

The Beast and the Vulture took their places on the cushions. Once seated, they could not turn their heads from side to side. They could only look straight ahead at their reflections in the mirror.

The purpose of this exercise was for them to look past their physical image and connect behind that image to the soul's image, the inner self, to see the hurt they caused others and take responsibility for their actions. They were given hope. The guide informed them they could simply ask for help and it would be given to them. The sacred Oil of Clarity was anointed on the forehead of every person in the House of Mirrors on a daily basis.

The Vulture wondered how he could keep his hair weave in place without assistance. His facelift, which he had five years earlier, might need a touch-up.

The Beast retreated back to his days of military service in the war. Man against man, brain against brain. He recalled his glory days. His job was dangerous, and he saved many lives. He was pronounced dead many times. He was front-page news.

Regardless of all that, here they would sit—sit until they could look past their images. They had all the time in the world.

Beware pride!

The Mansion of Truth and Jubilation

THE OTHERS PROCEEDED to the Mansion of Truth and Jubilation. Outside the Hall of Recollection, a shiny white stretch limousine awaited them. As they entered the limo with its plush seats, they wondered about the mansion and what surprises this new experience would deliver.

The driver drove on a circular path around a mountainous road. Despite the height, they felt safe. Suddenly, there was an opening to the right. The limo stopped so they could gaze upon the complete site. It was a wonder to behold.

It was surrounded by gardens that were perfectly landscaped. From the limo, they could inhale the unforgettable scent of flowers. The limo driver moved farther up the road.

There, in its magnificent splendor, stood the Mansion of Truth and Jubilation. It could not be placed in any particular architectural style. Very tall columns supported the upper balcony. The mansion looked very inviting—they felt drawn to enter. Three steps led to the wrap-around porch. Before they reached the top step, the doors opened. The Innocent Lamb, the child Dolores, could not contain her joy. She welcomed them with open arms.

As they entered, their eyes were fixed upon the middle staircase. It was made of white marble. The foyer was huge. They heard running water from the various fountains. The windblown chimes created feelings of tranquility. In this heavenly atmosphere, much healing would take place.

The Innocent Lamb's mother hugged her. Her eyes were filled with tears. She did not mean to hurt her child. Mother begged her for forgiveness. She said she needed help and medication. She didn't know how to be a mother. As they hugged, Mother whispered, "You are my cub."

Aunt came to her next. She was sorry she allowed the incestuous attack to continue. She could not imagine something like this happening. It was too horrible. Aunt sobbed as she told the Innocent Lamb she could not face the truth. Facing the truth would require her to take action. She was not ready for that.

The Innocent Lamb saw Father Uncle. He was wearing a white T-shirt and gray pants. He was young. She remembered the Father Uncle of her youth. His beautiful blue eyes were sparkling; his dark brown hair had not a strand out of place. He smiled and said, "Dolores, do you remember the Easter I brought home four little chicks for you and Grandma?" They both laughed and hugged.

The familiar smell of cherrywood tobacco meant only one thing. She turned, and Father was there. He was young and smiling. The cleft on his chin distinguished him the most. Their eyes met. Everyone laughed as he asked, "Where is the coffee?"

The woman who happened to be a nun reached out to the Innocent Lamb. She never meant to hurt her. In fact, she thought she was motivating her by calling her stupid.

The man who happened to be a priest could not face her. He felt shame and guilt. The Innocent Lamb sat with him while he related his story. His sister was impregnated at sixteen by a married man. They grew up in a strict Catholic family. His sister had to put the baby up for adoption. The parents demanded this of her. Once his sister saw the baby, she wanted desperately to keep him. After she gave him up, she was never the same. She committed suicide. When the Innocent Lamb came into the confessional, the priest was still angry and grieving the loss of his sister. He realized his words were harsh to the Innocent Lamb. By then, it was too late to find her. Throughout the years, he felt so much guilt over that. The Innocent Lamb hugged him. In her sweet manner, she told him all was forgiven.

This was a place of honest sharing, understanding, forgiving, and compassion for one another. The heart of the Innocent Lamb was filled with joy as she heard their stories (it was not her fault). She finally understood that others could give only what they had to give.

Suddenly, she heard crying from the last secret. He was sitting alone with both his hands covering his face. She walked over to him. It was just as she thought. He was corrupted by the Beast. This was the first time he spoke about his ordeal. It was all one big family secret. She listened and felt compassion for him. He was an Innocent Lamb too.

They would continue on their spiritual healing through the many rooms on the first floor. First was a conference room where they would begin their healing. Each was assigned a guide. Their astrological and numerology charts were explained to them. Then, their akashic records were opened. These records contained the soul journey of many lifetimes. They would retain their guides until they could trust their gut feelings and navigate on their own.

There was a therapy room, a conscience-clearing room, a writing room, a music room, and a library. The rest and relaxation area and the self-care rooms were required. They were given all the help they needed to heal. They were ready to go forward,

They had many rooms that they could revisit from time to time. Truth could not be acknowledged in one sitting. Healing did not run in a straight line. There were valleys, hills, mountains, and comfortable sure-footed roads. Truth changed as more was revealed.

The next phase of healing was energy healing. The Innocent Lamb learned about energy blocks in the body. Her life contained much trauma. She learned that this energy from her past could create blocks in her body—blocks that would prevent her success.

She started Reiki and acupuncture. She learned about the chakra system of the body and how imbalances would affect moving forward. They all started on the journey to healing.

The Innocent Lamb left the mansion early one morning. The dew still rested on the grass. She stood mesmerized by the sights around her. The bees were busy pollinating; the butterfly gently spread its wings, showing off the beauty of its transformation. Everything around her felt so alive. She listened; it was the sound of her favorite bird, the chickadee. Its song repeated its name: *chick-a-dee, chick-a-dee.*

Despite wanting to remain in the tranquility of this atmosphere, she was eager to continue on her spiritual quest. She looked up and saw a banner gently floating in the air. The words read, "Pathway to the Divine." Her thoughts manifested her desires very quickly.

She walked toward the banner. With each step, her feet touched the greener-than-green blades of grass. The banner led her to a bridge. She could not see what was beyond the bridge. Crossing the bridge was an act of faith.

The wooden bridge did not have a huge expanse. Its purpose was for soul questioning. On one side were questions to ponder. On the other were seats built into the side of the bridge to stop, write, and meditate.

Under the bridge, swans floated on the lake. She loved the swans. They glided across the water with the gracefulness of a ballerina pivoting on a stage. Their webbed feet working tirelessly under the water to move them forward remained unnoticed.

She took her first step across the bridge. The first question appeared. *Can you think with your heart—the heart beating rhythmically to support life and unconditional love?* To love, very simply, was the purpose of a spirit-guided life.

The next question appeared. *What are your intentions?* Did she operate from the desires of her ego, for glory and recognition? She did think about those things, but her intention for her work was pure—to help others. The less she possessed, the freer she would feel. The abundance would manifest on its own.

As she tried to concentrate on the questions, she was frequently distracted by the light that shone off the water. She was not in a hurry, savoring every moment—allowing her senses to bathe in the beauty of nature. Additional questions followed.

Can you sit in the silence to hear the message? After the death of her husband, she complained about loneliness. She realized loneliness was her choice. Happiness was her choice. When she started her writing project, she was so focused on the writing that she didn't have the energy to pursue social engagements. Then the a-ha moment. This was not loneliness. It was living in the silence. The silence was necessary for the growth of her soul.

Are you willing to go to any lengths to know God?

Many years ago, during the dark period of her life, she equated God with suffering. Now, she equated God with love. She made a commitment to God to follow her divine contract. The constant vigilance of her thoughts and actions would bring her closer to God.

Are you prepared for your greatest challenge? Can you live in the world by your principles?

Her answer*: I will take one day at a time.*

The last sign. Having reached this point, she was ready for the next step. The next step required a leap of faith. She was not afraid. Instead, she was thrilled, anticipating the wonderful surprises of the universe. Taking the leap of faith, she stepped into the darkness. Suddenly, a brilliance of such magnitude emerged. The ground was shining from the cut diamonds encrusted into the cement. Everything was sparkling like so many stars on a cloudless night.

Right in front of her stood the Tower of the Sacred and Divine. Surprisingly, it was a modern skyscraper, expanding its way up into the clouds. Standing in awe of the magnificence of this building, she felt the emanation of sacred vibrational energy. She felt the need to say a prayer.

Prayer of Commitment

Dear God,

I commit myself totally to you, seeking to do your will. Keep me focused on my journey, lest I become entrapped by success. Give me the energy to put my thoughts into actions. Fill me with your light. I entrust all to you. I thank you in advance.

Two trumpeters in golden robes stood in front of the huge glass entrance. As she walked toward the doors, the trumpeters greeted her with an enchanting melody.

Entering the ground level, she was entranced by the familiar scent of incense. A savory combination of burnt wood, spices, and charcoal brought back memories of the religious experiences of her youth. She stood there for a moment and closed her eyes, and with each breath, her body absorbed the intensity of the experience.

She opened her eyes and noticed an enormous book with gold lettering and binding. As she thumbed through the pages, she was familiar with many of the teachings.

She took the elevator to the first floor: self-love. The doors opened to a vast area where people were talking in groups. Immediately, they welcomed her. She listened to the other people sharing before it was her turn to speak.

Looking back over the years, she realized that living life on life's terms without using drugs or alcohol never afforded her self-love. Her compulsive overeating addiction always prevented her from loving herself.

As a child, kids made fun of her, calling her Fatso and Jelly Belly. They would hit her. She came home crying. Her grandmother told her she would have to defend herself. She was just five years old. She was told never to start a fight. Her grandmother always told her she was strong, not fat. Brother Uncle—she called him brother because he was about fifteen years older than her—taught her how to fight. After that, she never came home crying. Later, kids called her the Ox.

From the age of sixteen to thirty-three, she took amphetamines. With speed, her weight remained constant. Once she gave up the drugs and alcohol, the pounds started to accumulate. After her first year of sobriety, she started going to Overeaters Anonymous. It was not easy for her because of her defiance. Overeaters Anonymous required a lot of work. This was not a diet program. At the time, they offered a food plan called Gray Sheet Abstinence (now they have Dignity of Choice). It required three meals a day, zero in between, one day at a time (3-0-1). She was to eliminate sugars and white flour products. It was recommended when shopping to walk around the perimeter of the supermarket so that she would not be tempted by trigger foods. She felt hopeless enough to give herself to this program.

She used the tools of the program. She got a sponsor, wrote her food down in a journal, made phone calls, attended meetings, and wrote. She heard that there was no food that tasted as good as abstinence felt and that thin was not necessarily well. For breakfast, she ate half a cantaloupe and a plain yogurt. Her lunch was one cup of vegetables and three ounces of protein. Dinner was one cup of lettuce, one cup of vegetables, and three ounces of protein. Everything was weighed and measured. For three weeks, the hunger pains persisted. The weight came off. She lost fifty pounds.

Her pattern was to gain and lose fifty to sixty pounds. When she left Overeaters Anonymous to try other programs, they would work for a time. She punished her body by fasting. Once she got into sugar, she couldn't stop eating. She never had a blackout from her food addiction. She named herself the Shark. When she was into her addiction, she would devour anything and everything in sight. It was just like the alcohol—only she didn't have to drink alcohol. Food was necessary for the body. It was social, traditional, and comforting—it was so many things.

At night, she stood in front of the refrigerator, knowing that the emptiness in her gut would not be satisfied with anything in there. She was starving—but for what? She could not overcome the necessity of opening the refrigerator and trying to find some food that would satisfy her for that moment. At these times, she thought about her mother. Her mother was a night eater who made hero sandwiches early in the morning. Sometimes, she worried that she was just like her mother and would die just like her from compulsive overeating. That was not what was on the death certificate. The underlying cause of her mother's death was being obese. She wondered if her desire for love from her mother had kept her in the grips of a food addiction.

She put her scale in the trunk of her car. Doing this prevented her from weighing herself when she got up, with clothes on or without her clothes, before a bowel movement, after a bowl movement. The never-ending merry-go-round tormented her.

She was a good or bad girl by what she ate. The number on the scale dictated whether she was happy or sad. If she was happy, she celebrated and ate. If she was sad, she felt frustrated and ate. No matter what—she always ate. This was the insanity of her addiction.

Every time she weighed in at a diet program, she wore the same clothes. She took off her gold watch because it might add to her weight.

At times she left Overeaters Anonymous to look for an easier way. The pattern was always the same—try other methods, lose the weight, and gain it and more back.

She also tried hypnotism and past-life regression. She thought that her weight problem stemmed from a previous lifetime. She was hypnotized, and the answer that came to her was that the answer was within her. No one was to blame.

She tried gluten-free meals, meals prepared and delivered to her home, and numerous nutritionists. She took a basal metabolism test and checked her blood type to try the blood type diet. She tried others—too many to mention.

No matter how many things she accomplished, if her weight was high, nothing else mattered. Her self-esteem was based upon a number on the scale. For the longest time, she thought a 14W meant *wide* not *woman*.

She was thrilled with the bra extension. Putting on pantyhose was another matter. Her husband asked her what she was doing. She said, "It's karate!" This was how she was able to stretch the hose. She would have to sit on the bed, put the arch of the foot in, slowly stretch and pull the hose over the calf, then stand up, pull and squat, front kick, back kick, and squat again. It was always the lighter shades that gave her the most problems. She never bought queen size. She considered herself a princess.

Sitting on an airplane made her worry about her size. *What are the people sitting next to me thinking? Am I impinging on their space?* She would beat herself up for her lack of self-control regarding food.

Booths and cushioned seats at restaurants were a source of embarrassment. *Are my hips so wide that I might move the table as I get up?*

When she went out with friends, she hardly ate anything—only to go home and binge. To hide her eating, she ate while driving. She would have to run out in the middle of the night because the craving for sweets was just too much to resist. An invitation to a wedding in a few weeks or a few months made her think that she could lose some weight. Every time she saw a picture of herself, she could not believe it was her. She maintained a strong mentality. While she had so much in her life—a wonderful husband, a beautiful home—nothing mattered.

Even though she wasn't drinking or drugging, she didn't feel good about herself. Food was another drug.

Then there was the "someday when" thinking. *Someday when I lose twenty pounds, I'll go to the beach. Someday when I am a smaller size, I'll take that vacation. I'll attend that class. I'll go to the gym.* But that "someday" never came.

The "mañana syndrome" was simple: she would start her diet tomorrow because those sweets looked good tonight. This kept going for another day, another week, and she gained more weight.

She realized she needed to make peace with herself—not the food.

She started with an exercise of looking at herself in the full-length mirror. She told herself how beautiful she was. When she gazed into her eyes, tears fell. It was so hard to see herself at 217 pounds. She vowed that what she ate, her size, and the number on the scale would not dictate who she was. Her soul was what made her eyes glow. It had nothing to do with food.

She looked at her stomach and thanked her stomach for its gut feelings that directed her—feelings that were always right. She thanked her legs, although she could see some veins and cellulite. Despite it all, she was still standing. Those legs supported her. In the final analysis, it all came down to self-love and knowing that she was enough.

She desperately wanted to accept and love herself just as she was at that moment. For her entire life, she had struggled with the concept of self-love. She wondered if she had ever loved anyone. How could she love herself if she equated being heavy with hate? She started thinking differently about being heavy. It became clear as she spent time meditating on the word *heavy* that being heavy was a part of her.

Heavy provided her with protection. It was a barrier for intimacy. While she desired to be loved and intimate with a man, her past experiences were very hurtful. This was in her past. At this point in her life, she equated heaviness with hiding. Hiding was no longer necessary. The Wizard was here to protect her, to comfort her, and to be aware of her vulnerability. She wrote letters to her unconscious mind to release her heaviness and to achieve a healthy weight.

Sometimes she read the personals ads. Men wanted women who were financially secure and who were a certain size. They must be fit, must be thin. She didn't need a man to claim her. She claimed herself. In fact, she was thinking of placing an ad. *Looking for a six-sensory man. If you don't know what that means, don't waste my time.* She decided that what other people thought about her was none of her business. Once she started thinking like that, she felt so free. She was free to be herself without the approval of others.

She was perfect just the way she was at that moment. As a child of God, she was perfect. That divine spark (her soul) identified her to the Creator. From that soul spark, she was perfect.

Being around people who were just like her gave her comfort. A large percentage of food addicts were molested. Most people who were molested either became promiscuous (as she had) or never allowed themselves to be touched.

Never to trust, to her, was like not being human. The boundary issues. Just how far did one go to hug a child without infringing on that child's boundaries? What were her boundaries? All these issues appeared on the menu of molestation.

She vowed never to put her body through any more unhealthy diet rituals.

She became her own best friend, treating herself with understanding, kindness, and compassion. It was great to put herself first on the list of amends. Her friends were people who kept her best interests at heart. She let go of energy-draining, negative people. This process was difficult, but it was necessary to move forward. She was determined to eliminate any blocks that were holding her back from achieving her heart's desire.

Laws of the Universe
and Ego

It was important to distinguish the Laws of the Universe versus man-made laws. Universal laws were unchanging, while man-made laws were subject to change.

She studied the Law of Attraction. Now she was interested in the Law of Cause and Effect. In simple terms, the Law of Cause and Effect stated her actions toward others would come back to her. In biblical terms, it was "What ye sow, so shall ye reap." This law gave birth to the words *karma, karmic debt,* and *reincarnation.* Thinking along the laws of karma and reincarnation made forgiving easy. Without forgiveness, there would be no growth of the soul. Part of forgiveness was the letting go of the expectations she had of others. In doing so, she let go of the unrealistic expectations she had for herself.

She liked to think of her life as a play. All the actors were chosen before she came to the Earth School. Everyone had a role to play. Her thinking could change fate and destiny. Karmic debt could not be changed—it must be fulfilled.

When she complained about her mother, she realized that she chose her mother before she came to earth.

She pondered the following:

1) Did Christ have past lifetimes before He became the Master?
2) Were new souls being born or were old souls coming back to pay their karmic debt?

3) Would the end of the world occur when all souls had fulfilled their karmic debt?

She hoped that the answers would come while she traveled through the Tower. Whatever she needed, the universe delivered. It could be through a person (when the student was ready, the teacher appeared), a book, a bumper sticker, a dream, or even an e-mail. She felt she was both student and teacher.

Her gut feeling was directing her to the study of the ego (EGO in AA meant "Eases God Out"). At one time, she confused ego with self-esteem. Her ego was bisected in-depth through her study of Kabbalah with a spiritual teacher.

The ego was given to her at birth. The ego operated at a very subtle and powerful level. She found it was powerful only to the level she gave it power. Unless someone was aware, a person could live a whole life through the ego. The ego filled her with fear—most of which was created by other people's opinions of her. But she could now not forget the superficial emptiness of the so-called values embraced by man.

She had a meeting with a literary attorney. He said, "Do you know the odds that are against you for a first-time writer to publish a book?" She answered, "Do you know the odds of me still standing?" He responded, "Do you know you are going to meet a real live literary agent?" She answered, "Does she know she is going to meet a real alcoholic?" She was not deterred by these questions.

Without reading any part of her manuscript, the agent told her that, as a first-time writer, she needed to hire a ghostwriter. Again, another roadblock. Her guts were on the pages of her manuscript. A ghostwriter was unnecessary.

She left that meeting discouraged, but she would never give up. Overcoming difficult situations in her life had led her to this moment. Her faith and persistence would see her through.

The next literary agent she spoke to was at a literary convention. The agent asked, "Is that about abuse? Publishers have had it up to here with abuse. If you were a celebrity or a celebrity's daughter, a publisher would publish your book. I advise you to self-publish."

She knew that she would transcend the prophecies of mere mortals. Connecting to her divine spirit, she tapped into the living spring of God's power. God was her promoter. She was responsible for the effort—not the outcome. The outcome was in God's hands.

God started a good work in her, and he would complete it. "If God be for me, who can be against me?" She believed that God was delighted with her because of her childlike faith and her sense of humor.

Her Kabbalah teacher warned her about the opponent (evil, Satan, and obstacles).

Fatigue and insomnia bombarded her throughout her project. She argued with God. *How much more? You can't just talk the talk—you must walk the walk.* She looked at obstacles as opportunities for spiritual growth. The spiritual person, wanting to connect with the divine, begged for more. The more obstacles, the more spiritual growth there would be. She knew this was true through her life story.

She considered the criticisms of these people as part of the ego. It was negative energy to keep her from her dreams. It would try to limit her, to prevent her from achieving her greatest good. The ego diminished her. The ego cried to her from the voices of her past. The Cuckoo Bird. Did you just get up? The tramp. The drunk. The weak-willed, vulnerable, needy one. And she could go on and on. She refused to live in the negative with all she knew now.

She blasted her ego.

Her ego told her what she could not do.

She told her ego what she could do.

THE PENTHOUSE OF
SPIRITUALITY

SHE HEARD MANY rumors about living in the Penthouse of Spirituality. There was no pain, only love. This was her goal. It had taken her many lifetimes to reach this level.

She heard that here one could see over the rainbow. Spirituality replaced religion. Removing separateness and embracing all were one Unity replaced separateness competition no longer existed. There was sharing and cooperation. Every person was grateful for his or her unique talents. People were living in the present moment with perfect trust and perfect faith. They knew that all was provided and all was well. They recognized the goodness in one another.

There was no hell. God of all love could never create hell. Those who committed the worst crimes against humanity would face their hell— they would not see the face of God. They needed to come back many lifetimes to repay their karmic debt before they received their grace.

There were no mistakes. God did not make mistakes. How could she say that everything happened for a reason? There were no coincidences (God's way of remaining anonymous). Her decisions were based upon her life experiences up until that moment. Those who had no choice were the real addicts. There was a solution for them.

There was no security. Security was within. God was within. Poverty was man-made—not God-made. God offered the abundance of the universe. God was limitless. It was all in the *now*—she just needed to wake up to the freshness of the present moment.

She would feel the limitless and all-powerful connection to the Creator. She would claim power as a child of God. The ultimate was expressed in the words of St. Augustine: "Love God and do as you please." She would live in divine intimacy with God. She was grateful to be part of this age of transformation.

While she was contemplating the wonder of such an existence, a message interrupted her. Her presence was requested at the mansion. The others had completed their healing and wanted to celebrate. She rushed to the mansion. Opening the front door, she stood for a moment to behold the inner beauty of their souls. She could see their faces beaming with light.

Aunt heard the music first. Rushing up the marble staircase, they felt so light, as though they were flying. When they opened the huge doors, they were amazed at the beautiful ballroom. A full orchestra played music of every theme.

There was a circular dance floor. Beautiful tables, covered in fine linens, aligned the circle. A feeling of lightness and gaiety prevailed.

Looking up, an azure sky adorned with many sparkling stars replaced a roof. Aunt took her hand. She led her to the middle of the dance floor. She twirled her around and around. It was like old times—only better.

The dance? It was a Lindy, of course!

THE ULTIMATE LIFE BATTLE: THE FORCES OF LIGHT VERSUS THE FORCES OF DARKNESS

The Innocent Lamb was preparing for battle,
The Prince of Darkness and his cavalry
Versus the power of Light.
She turned to the Warrior Goddess
Athena, who was always by her side.
The Archangel Michael summoned the legions.
Now, this
Innocent Lamb, she wasn't stupid.
She lived her life by the golden key.
When she needed her power,
She went straight to the source,
The source of all power.
She reclaimed her power,
and
The Wizard was born.
Now
She has the power, the power over them all.

A new beginning,
Happy, joyous, and
free!

Is Debbie Married Yet?

So many men
They came to call
Some thin and some tall.
They called her name.
Made promises too,
Looked very lasting at the start,
But they left her with a broken heart.
She didn't spend much time to mend,
Started out searching again
For a man to fill that spot,
That spot we call the lonely heart.

Don't you know it's not the men
Who keep passing through again?
You have to look and take stock
Of what's really happening.

Oh, it's not outside you.
It's down deep within yourself.
Only you have the key
To unlock your lonely heart.
For all you Debbies out there,
Don't need a man,

At first to care.
Realize the beauty of your soul,
Then a man who is true
Will find his way to you.

And you ask
How do I know?
Because I was a Debbie too.

I AM NOT AFRAID

I am not afraid no more
To step outside my door
For so long I long to see
The other side of me
This is no easy fate
Coming from my place
Can I let my spirit soar
When I started from the floor
I must keep looking up
Oh EGO please shut up
There is this God part of me
Pulling setting me free
Finally finding my place
A part of the human race

My Epitaph

Here lies an ordinary person
Who, through the grace of God,
Accomplished extraordinary things.

Dolores Rose is a creative soul, a writer, and a motivator as well as an evolving spiritual person. She is a good listener. People find it easy to confide their life stories to her. Her path to spiritual growth was not an easy one. She struggled with abuse, addictions, and destructive behavior.

She reached bottom one dark weekend many years ago.

A survivor above all else, Dolores got the help she needed to change her life. Her vibrant sense of humor helped her through tough times.

Her heart's desire is to help other people through sharing her experience, strength, and hope. At first, she attempted to express her life through music. Without a musical background, she completed and produced one song, "Phony Diamond." She then turned to writing.

Her book, her memoir, is *I Have a Voice*.

Made in United States
North Haven, CT
06 February 2024

48413478R00055